MW01200361

With Me In Paradise

Lesson Learned from a Criminal

Eric D Tokajer

MDN

P.O. Box 10943

Pensacola, Florida 32524

ISBN 978-0-9894901-7-7

Published by:

MDN: P.O. Box 10943 Pensacola, Florida, 32524

Front cover design by: Eric Tokajer, Robin Harris, Catherine Currier and Hannah Wunder

All Scriptures are from the Tree of Life Version:

Table of Contents

3

Introduction

The pain was so excruciating he found himself wondering how he could still be conscious and aware of what was taking place around him. His mind questioned if he was awake. Was this reality or was he in a subconscious state in which his mind was working, but he was no longer actually experiencing things? Everything felt as if it was more of a dream than actual reality.

What he did know is that no matter if this was tangible or not he didn't want it to continue. The pain coursing through every part of his body was too unbearable. Each breath just kept adding to the enduring pain, while at the same time his body automatically forced itself to struggle through the agony for the next breath.

At first, he was able to see the crowd gathered to watch the execution and he listened to their insults and felt their spit and the objects as they hit his body. But after what seemed only seconds, everything blurred from his suffering; his reality became invisible while at the same time it also became nearly silent.

He knew in the back of his mind what was happening, but somehow, he found himself trying to rationalize a false narrative allowing him to block out the pain. Pain caused by each and every movement, no matter how small. Agony that brought him to the edge of unconsciousness only to find himself coming back to his senses. Just in time to press upward and gulp another breath.

From the very first moment he thought the pain was horrible. But it was impossible for a person to imagine the intensity of the pain that followed, which made the initial throbbing from the nails being driven into his hands and feet seem mild by comparison. First, the soldiers nailed him to the crossbeam. Afterwards, he was raised up and dropped with a loud thud into the resting place of the cross. While thinking his way through the process, he actually used the word resting-place in his mind and thought how ironic it was to use the word resting, in regards to anything involved with the method of execution called crucifixion.

The pain from the nails was tremendous. he agony caused

from the beam dropping into place on the cross-stand was horrible. But nothing could compare or prepare him for the intensity of the excruciating pain brought about by his body's natural fight for life, instinctively forcing itself to press against the nails and drawing up just enough to gasp one more breath into his lungs. A wrestling match inside of him, took place in between each agonizing inhalation, causing a war between his will to live and his desire to die. Yet, somehow, his flesh rose each time and fought for one more breath.

In his moments of lucidity, he would strain to open his eyes and ears to focus on what was happening around him. This was another survival mechanism his mind was using as an attempted distraction from the torture. Looking to his side, he saw another condemned man also writhing in pain, suffering in the same manner. He watched as he struggled, rising and falling with each strained breath. From his vantage point he was cognizant of the exertion being forced upon the other man's body, as the large nails caused tension which ripped against flesh and bone. He knew what he was seeing was a mirror of himself. Viewing what he could only previously feel happening somehow made the unbearable pain increase. He suddenly and dramatically came to realize he could not only feel what was happening to him, he was also able to watch.

He saw the man next to him push himself up, draw breath with great difficulty and exhale the words, "Father, forgive them, for they do not know what they are doing."
These words spoken with such feeling cut into his heart. How could a man in such agony ask for forgiveness for those who were responsible? Especially as this man was speaking those words, the very men who had nailed him on the cross were casting lots and dividing up His clothing?

He watched as an inscription was nailed to the beam above the man's head, *"This is the king of the Jews."*

He heard one man in the crowd sneer, *"He saved others; let Him save Himself if He is the Messiah of God, the Chosen One!"*

Moments later, one of the soldiers mocking him offered him sour wine to drink.

He looked beyond the man in the middle, the King of the Jews, to the condemned man on the other side of him. Previously aware of his presence, he heard his voice call out loudly saying,

"Aren't You the Messiah? Save Yourself—and us!"

These words jarred something inside of him, causing him to burn within, as they permeated his soul. They seemed to echo within, as if they actually were bouncing around between his head and his heart.

Messiah!

King!

Salvation!

Could he really be?

In an instant, his questions were answered. Not by a voice from heaven calling forth as it did from Mount Sinai. But a still, small voice within his spirit. It wasn't a shout but a whisper; no less impactful, powerful and real.

He heard the words of rebuke.

"Don't you fear God, since you are under the same

sentence? We're getting what we deserve for our actions, and rightly so—but this One has done nothing wrong."

It was with great surprise he realized those words had come out of *his* mouth. He continued speaking with complete faith saying,

"Yeshua, remember me when You come into Your kingdom."

Yeshua answered, and spoke words of overpowering hope. They overcame the intensity of the pain:

"Amen, I tell you, today you shall be with Me in Paradise."

He was not sure how, but at that moment, in the middle of his torment, as his very limbs were being ripped from their joints, for the first time he felt a unique blend of freedom, joy and peace. He once again pressed himself to rise up.

Not just in effort to gasp another breath. This time he pressed himself through the pain so he could raise himself up to worship his God.

He had never felt so much. The truth? He didn't have words to describe what he was feeling. Everything changed inside of him. He felt clean and new. His anger and hatred were gone and he understood how this man next to him, this man who he now knew was more than just a man. He knew he was the long awaited Messiah of Israel.

This is the Messiah religious leaders were always speaking about; the one who would restore Israel to the glory she had when Solomon ruled.
The one who would cause the wolf and the lamb to dwell together and bring perfect peace to the earth.
The one, who from Jerusalem, would rule and reign not over not only Israel but over the whole world.

While these thoughts were spinning through his mind, he noticed out of the corner of his eye, a Roman soldier walking towards him.

This sight shook him out of his thoughts and suddenly caused him to remember where he was, what was happening and with that realization the immense pain returned in full.

The soldier stood in front of him at the foot of the cross. He saw a club being swung in his direction. He felt the impact as his legs were broken.

He didn't understand how this could happen at this moment? How was it that at the moment when he found his Messiah, when in the depths of his heart, faith was born, a time when he not only understood freedom from his shame and sin but, knew he had received complete forgiveness and newness of life.

This moment, filled with swelling emotion, which he had not felt since his childhood, would end in death in just minutes with his legs broken.

His last moments on earth were filled with these questions and then suddenly... standing in front of him was Yeshua in all His glory. His arms open wide with welcome. His eternity had begun and Yeshua's promise, made on the cross, was fulfilled. He was, that day in Paradise with Yeshua.

The criminal's execution described above took place and was included as an integral part of what is one of the most important events ever to take place on Earth. In the middle of the crucifixion of Yeshua, when the King of all Kings is offering himself as a redemptive sacrifice for the world, we find included dialogue between Yeshua and the two criminals who were being executed with Him.

###

The scene was one I had experienced many times over my 20+ years as a rabbi. I was in a hospice center with a family spending the last few moments with their loved one. The only difference, this time I was a part of the family and the loved one was my mother.

This time, instead of being the one providing comfort and answering the questions, I was the one searching for answers. Heartbroken, I was in pain, and in a weird way, lost. I felt abandoned when the last breath left her body.

In my world, where everything is based upon God and family, the epicenter was no longer there. The questions of who, what, why and how streamed through my mind with such speed, I could not even begin to consider the ramifications of one before the next question arose. Each question built upon the other until I was certain my mind was spinning in my skull.

The more I tried to think, the less I was able. The more questions I attempted to answer, the answers more distant.

This was not the first family death I had experienced but it was the first to affect my emotional, personal, spiritual and social equilibrium.

The day came unexpectedly. Only weeks before, my mother seemed to be a healthy, energetic 72-year-old woman. We had just attended a Bat Mitzvah together in North Carolina and were driving back together to South Florida. While at the Bat Mitzvah, my mother said she was not feeling well and by the time we reached Atlanta, Georgia her difficulty breathing had arisen to the level of emergency. We brought her to the hospital. She had a battery of tests and was discharged with instructions to see her doctor at home. We drove the rest of the way from Atlanta to her home in the Villages, Florida. Within days she was in a hospice center and within 3 weeks, she was gone.

Throughout the process, I cried out in prayer over and over. Searching my heart for anything within me that might keep my prayers from being answered, I went through the normal process of trying to make deals with God and pleading with Him for her health and life to be restored.

To make this time even more confusing, after years of praying for my mother to accept Yeshua as the Messiah, in the midst of these last days she not only accepted Him, but with joy through her pain, proclaimed her faith enthusiastically to everyone and anyone who would listen.

On one of our last mornings together, I entered her room. To my delight, she was sitting up and smiling.
I asked, "How are you feeling?"
"I am wonderful," she said with enthusiasm, "I spent all last night talking with my Messiah."

Following her profession of faith in Yeshua as Messiah, my expectation grew and in my mind. I began to visualize her healed, coming home, and spending years together experiencing our relationship together as Messianic Jews.

The next day, however, her health worsened and on the next afternoon, she left this world for the world to come. Outwardly, I was a rock of faith. I was after all, a rabbi and my family, both those who believe in Yeshua and those who did not, needed me for spiritual guidance and comfort.

When I was asked the usual litany of why questions, I provided the same answers I had given to so many other families throughout my ministry. Even though every answer I provided was Biblically accurate, somehow, this time, they seemed hollow and meaningless. I don't mean to say I didn't believe what I was saying, nor was my faith shattered or even shaken.

I knew the answers I provided were correct. However the questions that day were still more powerful than the answers.

It would be nice to be able to say that after a short time in prayer the answers to all of my questions came quickly to me. However, I cannot. It was years later when I actually understood. The answers, ironically, came to me while searching for different answers to different questions, arising from someone I loved who suffered through the worst experience imaginable.

I believe the delay in my receiving my answers was not because God did not or would not answer me. I fully believe at the time of my mother's death, God was attempting to answer my questions.

But I was too busy grumbling, complaining and questioning to listen to His voice.

It would be impossible to write a book to answer all the questions to the "whys" we, as believers, have in life. Each person, no matter how similar the situation, will have different questions based on their own experiences.

This book is my way of sharing the answer I received to my question of "why." I know it will not provide every answer to every question. However, it will provide a scriptural road map for the spiritual journey needed to find the answers. Reading through the book, notice information at times may seem redundant. Please understand a pattern that is repetitive in the Scriptures is by necessity, needed to be recurring. It is also my hope for those who read this book to learn the pattern and apply it to their walk with God, so they may live within the entirety of the blessings He has promised to His people.

One day, while I was reading through this series of verses in the Book of Luke, Chapter 23, I began to ponder about the inclusion of the interactions between the criminal and Yeshua at the crucifixion.

I came to realize, if one only wanted to accurately portray the details of the death of Yeshua they could have done so without providing any of the details or involvement of these two men. After all, Yeshua was being unjustly killed for both religious and political reasons. The two criminals executed along with him were guilty of their crimes. Including the convicts and their interactions seemed superfluous. If this conversation had been left out of the story, it would not have changed anything about His death.

It was Yeshua who was the focus of attention and it was His death that provided the required offering for sin. Beyond the comparison of the two sinners verses the one savior really didn't appear to offer any real value.
Why was the narrative of these two men included? I asked myself.

We know there is nothing written in the Holy Scriptures added unnecessarily or as just an added bonus.

I began to pray and search, digging myself into the verses, to find out why these statements were inspired to be included.

After only a short amount of time it was clear to me. I found there were symbolic reasons to include the convicts at the site of the crucifixion. Their presence was to fulfill the Biblical prophetic types to connect the crucifixion with shadows from the Tanakh (Old Testament).

One example of these types and shadows is contained in the story of Joseph's dream interpretation while in prison, found in Genesis chapter 40:1:

Now it was after these things that the cupbearer and the baker of the king of Egypt offended their master, the king of Egypt.

Here we find Joseph innocent, convicted and in prison, along with the baker and cupbearer, both of whom were guilty.

Cupbearer:

40:8 They said to him, "We dreamed a dream and there is no one to interpret it." Then Joseph said to them, "Don't interpretations belong to God? Please tell me." **40:**9 So the chief of the cupbearers told his dream to Joseph, saying to him, "In my dream, suddenly, there was a vine in front of me. 40:10 On the vine were three branches, and as it was budding, its blossoms came out, its clusters ripened into grapes. 40:11 Pharaoh's cup was in my hand and I took the grapes, pressed them into Pharaoh's cup and put the cup in Pharaoh's palm." 40:12 "This is its interpretation," Joseph said to him. "The three branches: they are three days. 40:13 In another three days, Pharaoh will lift up your head and restore you to your position. Then you'll put Pharaoh's cup in his hand just as you used to do before when you were his cupbearer.

Baker:

40:16 When the chief of the bakers saw that the interpretation was good, he said to Joseph, "I also was in my dream. Expectantly, there were three baskets of white bread on my head. 40:17 In the top basket was

22

food for Pharaoh—all kinds of baked goods. But the birds were eating them from the basket on my head." 40:18 Then Joseph answered and said, "This is its interpretation. The three baskets: they are three days. 40:19 In another three days Pharaoh will lift up your head—off of you—and will hang you on a tree. Then the birds will eat your flesh off of you."

As we read on, we see the Cupbearer was to be given life while the Baker received death. A clear connection can be seen between the two criminals who were in prison with Joseph and the two criminals crucified with Yeshua.

In both cases, one innocent and two guilty. We also see in both situations, one was set free and one condemned to death.

Another type is found in Genesis Chapter 22:

3 So Abraham got up early in the morning, saddled his donkey and took two of his young men with him, and Isaac his son. He split wood for the burnt offering, and got up and went to the place about which God had told him.

Isaac walked toward his own sacrifice with two men as he was to be offered by his father Abraham.

On a side note, please notice the usage of three days, a type and shadow which we are not going to discuss here, but is important to notice as we discuss types and shadows and prophetic connections between events in Tanakh and fulfillments in the New Testament.

These foreshadowing events, like so many others, were provided as signs and precursors in the Torah for Israel to remember and prepare to receive the coming of Yeshua.

To me, these symbolisms initially seemed like a good enough reason for the inclusion of the two men at Yeshua's crucifixion. After all, they bring into view types and shadows, familiar to the people of Israel from Torah, specifically designed for the people of Israel to recognize of whom and what Yeshua was, when he was lifted up before them.

But even with the symbolism of types and shadows, I felt as if there had to be a much deeper reason for the interaction at such an important moment in time. After all, the type and shadow connection could have been accomplished without any conversation taking place. The two men with Isaac were silent and the Scriptures only revealed their presence.

Think about it. These few hours of time, marked in the history of the world, was the climax of everything God set into motion at the very foundation of Earth. From before the very first "Let there be…," the plan for this moment was preordained. In this place, and at this critical juncture in time, God's plan was to include these two criminals on that hill, in that city, with Messiah.

Taking place at the exact moment, when Yeshua is paying the ultimate payment for sin, when all eyes should be on Yeshua and all ears listening to his last words, instead of fully focusing our attention on Him only, we are focusing upon *three* men nailed to their cross, having discourse.

Everything within us should scream, *'there has to be more!'* There must be a greater reason to include this exchange of words between these men. Just think about the effort it took to even have conversation. The energy involved in rising up to gasp for just enough oxygen, then dropping down to expel air while forcing words out of parched lips.

I thought, there just had to be more meaning, more than just a type and shadow. Somehow in the discourse, God had to be saying something vitally important. The moment was too great for anything to fall short of world changing. I began to look at these verses from different angles, probing for a profound message hidden in plain site within the text. Then it happened. A pattern appeared and though I'd spent years studying God's word, I had never seen it before. This pattern provides, for those who follow it a way to receive all of the blessings God promised His people within the pages of the Bible.

The "Whys" Questions:

1) Have you experienced a moment when your faith has been strong and yet you questioned why things were happening as they were?

2) What "Whys?" are in your life?

3) Have you found peace with your questions?

4) Did you look into the Bible for similar situations when you were trying to find your answers?

5) If so, give some examples you found during your search.

Patterns

Most students of the Bible realize God works through patterns. These patterns are seen throughout the Bible starting with the Creation account following a set structure, which God used to begin with "In the Beginning."

From the moment God called forth something from out of nothing, and continuing as He spoke the world into existence one item at time in an organized fashion, he used specific patterns.

The book of Isaiah 28:10 said it this way:

"For it must be 'precept upon precept, precept upon precept, line upon line, line upon line, here a little, there a little.'"

We see examples of these connections of text and pattern starting from the very beginning of Genesis to the end of the Revelation. One such example is the theme and importance of light.

The first mention is found starting in Genesis 1:3:

"Let there be light,"

The thread or web of verses teaching us about light and the symbolism of light continue throughout the text until Revelation 21:23 **_"And the city has no need for the sun or the moon to shine on it, for the glory of God lights it up, and its lamp is the Lamb,"_** and Revelation 22:5 **_"Night shall be no more, and people will have no need for lamplight or sunlight—for Adonai Elohim will shine on them. And they shall reign forever and ever."_**

Between Genesis 1:3 and Revelation 22:3-5 a continuing connective thread links together the first promise of the Messiah as the Light of the World with the fullness of the promise found last chapter of the Bible. When one starts at the beginning of this thread of verses and follows it to the completing verse, only then will they be able to see the full pattern established. Once the pattern is revealed we can comprehend the context of "light" in Scripture.

We can understand "light" was provided so we would know and understand the Messiah has always existed since before the foundation of the world.

Another example of the connective patterns through Scripture is what I call the "garden pattern." In the book of Genesis, we find Adam in the Garden of Eden and it was perfect and pure in every way. Through Adam's sin death entered the world. By Adam's rejection of God's will we find man's first defeat took place in a garden. Years later, Yeshua was in a garden submitting himself to the will of the Father in Mathew 26:39:

39 Going a little farther, He fell face down and prayed, saying, "My Father, if it is possible, let this cup pass from Me! Yet not as I will, but as You will.

This action of submission to God's will brought about the reversing of the actions of Adam.
As we read in Romans 5:12-20:

12 So then, just as sin came into the world through one man and death through sin, in the same way death

spread to all men because all sinned. 13 For up until
the Torah, sin was in the world; but sin does not count
as sin when there is no law. 14 Nevertheless death
reigned from Adam until Moses, even over those who
had not sinned in a manner similar to the violation of
Adam, who is a pattern of the One to come. 15 But the
gracious gift is not like the transgression. For if many
died because of the transgression of one man, how
much more did the grace of God overflow to many
through the gift of one Man—Yeshua the Messiah. 16
Moreover, the gift is not like what happened through
the one who sinned. For on the one hand, the judgment
from one violation resulted in condemnation; but on
the other hand, the gracious gift following many
transgressions resulted in justification. 17 For if by the
one man's transgression, death reigned through the
one, how much more shall those who receive the
overflow of grace and the gift of righteousness reign in
life through the One, Messiah Yeshua. 18 So then,
through the transgression of one, condemnation came
to all men; likewise, through the righteousness of one
came righteousness of life to all men. 19 For just as
through the disobedience of one man, many were

made sinners, so also through the obedience of one man, many will be set right forever.

This same concept is said another way in 1 Corinthians 15:45-49:

45 So also it is written, "The first man, Adam, became a living soul cf. Gen. 2:7. ." The last Adam became a life-giving spirit. 46 However, the spiritual is not first, but the natural; then the spiritual. 47 The first man is of the earth, made of dust; the second man is from heaven. 48 Like the one made of dust, so also are those made of dust; and like the heavenly, so also are those who are heavenly. 49 And just as we have borne the image of the one made from dust, so also shall we bear the image of the One from heaven.

In a garden, the first Adam lost the battle and it was in a garden the second Adam won the battle and brought restoration.

As we begin to notice the patterns within Scripture, we will start to view Scripture as more than a simple storybook, intended to lead us to faith in God and the Messiah. Rather, we find within its pages a very complex operating manual or instruction book for functioning within the universe both physically and spiritually.

I believe the conversation on the cross between Yeshua and the criminal at His side, provides for us a section of the architectural plans required to restore man and to repair a relational link to the promises of God in our lives. With this idea in mind, let's begin our study into the blueprint or plan known as the Bible.

The Hebrew Word *Torah,* can be defined as the first five books of the Bible, Genesis through Deuteronomy which are often referred to as The Law. In actuality the word *Torah* is defined as teachings or instructions. Yet most people never visualized the whole Bible as set of instructions or a technical manual. If the Bible is, in fact, a set of instructions provided by our Designer, wouldn't it stand to reason we should be able to follow those instructions or patterns in order to achieve the maximum design results?

These instructions should provide for us a format, governing not only all of our functions body, soul and spirit, but also our interactions with the rest of our world.

Said another way, if there is a designed order to the created universe and if we follow those instructions as given, then we will end up with the product operating as it was designed.

An important thought to insert here is the original design of our world and mankind is what we read about in the Garden of Eden and not what we have today. Remember too, the fall of Adam and Eve brought sin and death, which changed the operational status of all things. We also must realize Yeshua's life, death and resurrection brought not only deliverance, but also restoration. Through faith in Yeshua as Messiah, we can return to the optimum adherence of the instructions which will provide restoration to the original design.

For a long time, men have worked hard trying to restore both mankind and the world in which he dwells. Some of those who have tried used parts of the blue prints (The

Bible) and have, in many ways, been successful in restoring sections of the world. Others have tried to put things back into order without consulting the plan and the results have been a disastrous blend of false beliefs and superstitions.

In Judaism, this concept of the restoration of the world is called Tikkun Olam. It is taught that it is the responsibility of every follower of Judaism to involve themselves in repairing the world and each of us should live our lives in such a way that when we leave this world, the world will be made closer in some way to its original perfect state.

Like most people who come to faith, I began to read the Bible on a regular basis. My entry into Biblical studies provided me with more questions than answers. I read through the Bible and I consistently came upon questions for which I could not find answers. This was okay with me, because as a Jew, I had been taught the purpose of studying was not about finding conclusions but rather to seek even deeper questions. While it is true we will always find more questions, the problem I found was I didn't know the correct questions to ask.

I understood as fact God was the Creator and He framed the world in an organized fashion with intentionality. God is a master planner and designer. I knew He had blueprints for all His creation and it was possible for us to find those designs and follow patterns. Living a full and blessed life would be the result.

My questions didn't originate from concerns about what God said would happen. They consisted of why the things he said would happen were not happening in my life and the lives of many of the believers I knew. In other words, throughout the Bible God had made covenant promises with His people. These promises are irrevocable and unchangeable. Yet, I was not seeing them come to pass in my life or in the lives of those around me who were professing to be in covenant with God.

My questions didn't ask why in the direction of God. Instead I asked the questions in my direction. I knew beyond a shadow of a doubt God had given promises and I also knew He could not and would not break His word. So the answer to the question of why I was not seeing the fruition of the blessings promised in God's word had to be

36

something I was not understanding or doing or fulfilling on my side of the covenant agreement.

This book is the result of years of searching for answers to one of life's most difficult questions. The question: "Why we don't see God's promises fully taking place in our lives?" I would be less than honest if I told you I had found all of the answers to that question. I will say that in this book, I will share one pattern from the Bible, that although it won't answer every question concerning the blessing of God, it will help us to ask the right questions to one of the "why nots" in our lives.

It is my prayer that those who choose to read this book will gain a new perspective. Allowing them not only to ask the right questions about why, but also to follow the pattern leading to walking in the fullness of the promises God has given to each of us in His word.

This pattern, as with all other Biblical patterns, begins in the Book of Genesis and is seen over and over throughout the balance of the Bible. Once you see it, it becomes undeniable.

The Bible is full of patterns God included purposely for our understanding. The more we look for them the more we will see the web of patterns connecting the Scriptures in a way, which demonstrates the carefully orchestrated plan of God. These patterns are seen in the order and pattern of creation. They are visible in the design of all life; everything we know, see and touch has a formulated pattern which, when all is correct, follows the planned order.

In the Hebrew language, when someone asks how you are, a response is "beseder" or "in order." This Hebraic concept views one's life in terms of being in order or out of order. Every blessing we receive in life comes when things are in order and every bad thing happens when something is out of order. Our very life begins when we follow the established design of reproduction. Death comes when our organs cease to function in their created order. Medical science has proven cancer is simply the existence of cells out of order within the body.

With this in mind, we realize the Bible is more than just words on page. It has a unique structural order, a master design. The whole of Scripture is an interconnected cellular structure, fashioned in the same way man was created, by God speaking it into existence.

I know that you may have read that last statement and said to yourself, 'Didn't God form Adam from clay of the earth and then form Eve from Adam's side?' Of course He did. He did so from the structure He spoke into being, He breathed the breath of life into man, in the same fashion that He breathed the words that formed all of creation.

The design of the Bible is as purposely complex as the everything else created. As human bodies consist of a DNA pattern, Scriptures are also formed together in a distinct pattern. When we read the words from Isaiah 28:10:

"For it must be 'precept upon precept, precept upon precept, line upon line, line upon line, here a little, there a little.'"

This phrase isn't referring to simple paragraph or sentence structure, as it is often misconstrued, but it is described to a much deeper reality.

Each and every syllable of each word is structural and part of a perfectly designed pattern spoken into existence by God.

Once grasped, we can then start to align ourselves with the patterns provided so we can begin to dwell within the patterns. These patterns provide instructions to walk in the fullness of the promises enshrined within the Bible. These promises are available to everyone, as long as they follow the patterns.

Once we see them, we begin noticing them everywhere. Some appear simple and others will be much more complex. The more you see the more you will understand each pattern was built into the text as a part of the continuity of purposeful design.

Each and every line of Biblical text was written to layout these patterns, and the interwoven patterns together provide for us an instructional document, which when followed, allows us to function in our fullest. The Bible refers to this in Psalm 16:11:

You make known to me the path of life. Abundance of joys are in Your presence, eternal pleasures at Your right hand.

Many books have been written demonstrating some of these patterns. Books about the Tabernacle design as it pertains to and describes the plan of redemption, The Jewish Wedding as it shows the joining together of and the calling out of believers. The Biblical Feast Days and their fullness in the events of Messiah's birth, death, resurrection and return. Even the Exodus from Egypt which shows a pattern from God's call to those in the slavery of sin and their ultimate journey's end in the World to Come.

Many reading this book will have some understanding of the traditional Passover Seder (Passover meal) found in the Haggadah (Guidebook for the Passover meal) and the patterns demonstrated by the various elements; such as, the Lamb slain and blood covering, the matzah, the four cups of wine, the bitter herbs and even the Afikomin (Piece of matzah hidden and then searched for as part of the Seder). The pattern of the Seder clearly shows a pattern of the events of the death, burial and resurrection of Yeshua.

41

These are only a few of the many examples of the intricate patterns woven throughout the words of the Bible written under the unction of the Spirit as we read in 2 Peter 1:16:

"For we did not follow cleverly concocted tales when we made known to you the power and coming of our Lord Yeshua the Messiah, but we were eyewitnesses of His majesty. 17 For when He received honor and glory from God the Father, a voice came to Him from the Majestic Glory: "This is My Son, whom I love; with Him I am well pleased! 18 And we ourselves heard this voice come out of heaven, when we were with Him on the holy mountain. 19 Furthermore, we have the reliable prophetic word. You do well by paying attention to it, as to a lamp shining in a dark place, until the day dawns and the morning star rises in your hearts. 20 Above all understand this: no prophecy of Scripture comes about from a person's own interpretation. 21 For no prophecy was ever brought forth by human will; rather, people spoke from God as they were moved by the Ruach ha-Kodesh."

Notice, we are not only told the Scriptures are prophetic, but also that we would do well by paying attention to His word. We were provided within the Scriptures a uniquely interwoven web of patterns that make the design of the human body pale in comparison.

Just as human DNA can be dissected and studied to understand how each strand works, effects the whole and how each individual DNA strand unites to form the totality of the structure of a human body, individual words of the Bible each directly influence our understanding of the complete word. Each word, sentence and phrase contributes to patterns helping us to interact with our Creator and His Word, in a way that brings fullness to our relationship. Light shines upon the pathway God desires for us to walk through, providing clarity when we understand the patterns He reveals to us in His word. When we do so, we open the door to the blessings He has promised His people in the very words we are studying.

The pattern I'm sharing is based upon familiar verses I've read over and over for many years. One day while studying, a nugget or revelation appeared to me, almost as a hologram would appear before your eyes. The words seemed to stand out of the page as if they were highlighted. I don't want this to seem too supernatural or even unusual to those reading this, because I know everyone who reads the Scripture has the same or similar experience as the words or verses become alive and personally relevant to us.

I immediately started to make mental notes of what I had seen within the words so I would have a file saved in my mind to share this nugget with my congregation. I was excited about being inspired by the words, especially since this particular nugget was one I thought could help people in their walk with God.

Many of the things we learn while studying are interesting and inspirational but they are also knowledge that at times has impact on our soul, but not always on our lives. To clarify this, I must say it is very meaningful to understand that the definitions of the first ten names in the linage from Adam to Noah share the message of the Gospel. But even though it is interesting and valuable, it doesn't immediately impact my life in a significant way.

The names in order are.

Adam -Man

Seth -Appointed

Enosh – Mortal

Kenan – Sorrow

Mahalalel – The blessed God

Jared – Shall come down

Enoch – Teaching

Methuselah – His death shall bring

Lamech – Despairing

Noah – Comfort and rest

If you place each of those meanings into a complete sentence here is the sentence it forms:

Man, appointed, mortal, sorrow, the blessed God, shall come down, teaching, His death shall bring, despairing, comfort and rest.

The above names and their individual and combined definitions definitely confirm the orchestration of the Bible and helps to establish the divine inspiration of every word.

It doesn't however provide keys for believers to by live in order to walk in the promises of God after one finds the One who would bring the rest and comfort promised.
The nugget or pattern I received and which I am sharing in this book, has the ability, if received, to help people understand how to live within the fullness of the promises of God.

The pattern is found hidden right in front of our eyes as we read about what is happening to the criminal on the cross next to Yeshua and the powerful conversation that takes place between those two men. This conversation was not simply about one man, who in the last moments of his life finds redemption through the words of the Messiah of Israel. The dialogue holds within its few short phrases the final lesson shared vocally and visibly by Yeshua to not just those watching that day but to all who will ever read His words. In The Book of John chapter 19 we read the following:

30 When Yeshua tasted the sour wine, He said, "It is finished!" And He bowed His head and gave up His spirit. 31 It was the Day of Preparation, and the next day was a festival Shabbat. So that the bodies should not remain on the execution stake during Shabbat, the Judean leaders asked Pilate to have the legs broken and to have the bodies taken away. 32 So the soldiers came and broke the legs of the first and then the other who had been executed with Yeshua. 33 Now when they came to Yeshua and saw that He was already dead, they did not break His legs.

Notice the conversation he had with this unnamed criminal took place just before he uttered the words, "It is finished," and "gave up His spirit." I believe the words, 'it is finished' apply not only to the redemptive work of Yeshua that provided a means of salvation for all who would place their trust in Him, but because those final words were spoken just after his final conversation, I believe 'it is finished' also applies to having completed this hugely significant interchange with this unnamed condemned man.

This dramatic lesson, taught at such an intense time, holds the key for every believer receiving the blessings promised by God to His people.

While this book could become an exhaustive study written on hundreds of pages, my goal is to write this book in a way that will serve to bless as many people as possible. With that goal in mind, and knowing that the majority of people are not theologians looking for a thesis paper, this book by design will cover only seven of the many examples in the Bible.

The hope being that many people will apply the principles provided in the revealed pattern to their lives, releasing access to the many blessings God has promised His people in the Scriptures. Secondly, I hope many of those who read the book will see the pattern so clearly they not only apply it to their personal lives but also teach it to others. Thirdly, it is desired for this book to lay the groundwork, for those who choose, to look further through the Scriptures to find more examples of patterns so all of God's people will live what God's word describes in John 10:10 as life more abundantly:

10 The thief comes only to steal, slaughter, and destroy. I have come that they might have life, and have it abundantly!

The Pattern Questions:

1) If God established patterns in his word for everything from Creation to His established families, do you think looking for patterns will help us grow in establishing His will for our lives?

2) What Biblical patterns have you found most applicable to your life?

3) Do you think patterns in Scripture can apply to more than on situation or subject?

4) When looking at physical patterns established in Scripture, do you believe there are always spiritual counterpart patterns?

5) Do you think all Biblical Patterns are universally applicable?

Irrevocable Patterns of Promise

As we will have begun to observe, there are no coincidences in the Bible. So it should not come as a surprise that in Yeshua's parable of the shepherd, we read about a thief who comes to steal, slaughter and destroy. Nor should it come as a surprise that Yeshua used a conversation with a thief or criminal to restore to His people abundant life.

The promises of God are many and varied and as we read through the Bible, we find them being spoken either directly by God or by the prophets of God. These promises begin with the very first four words that God spoke in Genesis Chapter 1:3-4:

3 Then God said, "Let there be light!" and there was light. 4 God saw that the light was good.

God speaks light into existence and with those words we have the absolute assurance that everything God says will happen will happen. Often when we read through these words we do so quickly, acknowledging God did speak these words and light exists because He did. But we do not always assign to these words the understanding and value they hold. Between His saying "Let there be" and reading "there was" an eternal truth planted was established for us all time. The truth is simple yet profound. God will do everything He says he will every time. For the believer, these words make it possible for us to have the confidence that each promise made throughout the Bible will come to pass. It is impossible for one to not believe, by the single act of God speaking, light, which was not, suddenly was. The fact when we wake up in the morning, open our eyes and see light should provide all of the evidence we need. God makes promises and even more importantly, He keeps those promises.

In the book of Numbers Chapter 23:19 we find this truth said in a different way by the Prophet Balaam:

19 God is not a man who lies, or a son of man who changes his mind! Does He speak and then not do it, or promise and not fulfill it?

These words spoken to King Balak are very important in our understanding of the promises of God, especially as they relate to today. Looking deeper into the context of these words, Balak was the king of Moab, a Gentile ruler who hired Balaam, a prophet of God to curse the children of Israel. In the context of this scripture, Balak has heard what has happened to the Amorites. Terror had come upon him and he knows Moab cannot defeat the children of Israel because Balak understood God was with them. The whole earth knew of the plagues of Egypt and the strong arm of the God of Israel.

Balak knows Balaam is a Prophet of God and is thinking as an idol worshipper would with many gods, which were arbitrary in their promise keeping. So he came up with the plan to ask God to change His mind and bring a curse upon Israel. Balak doesn't know the God of Israel cannot break a promise. He comes to Balaam as most pagans do, placing the power of God in the hands of men. We know this by the very words Balak speaks in Numbers 22:6:

6 Come now, curse this people for me, because they are too strong for me! Perhaps I may be able to defeat them and drive them away from the country. I know that whoever you bless will be blessed and whoever you curse will be accursed!

Notice Balak believes by asking Balaam to curse Israel, the God of Israel would simply change His mind and break His promises to Israel. Also, notice the similarity of the request of Balak to Balaam and the promise God had given to Abraham in Genesis 12:2-3:

2 *My heart's desire is to make you into a great nation, to bless you, to make your name great so that you may be a blessing. 3 I will bless those who bless you, but whoever curses you I will curse, and in you all the families of the earth will be blessed.*

You see the whole world at the time of Balak's conversation with Balaam knew the power of God, because of the ten plagues that came upon Egypt and the deliverance of the children of Israel. Balak knows God was with Israel and the only hope he had of defeating Israel was to get God to curse His children. The truth is that Balak's understanding of the situation was correct. The only hope Moab had in defeating Israel would be for God to bring a curse. The problem was not in the concept of blessings and curses; the problem was in the plan to bring about the curse. Balak thought by asking the prophet to speak curses over Israel God would simple change His mind and switch teams. Balak didn't understand the absolute God cannot lie or change His mind. Balaam's answer to Balak was simple and straightforward. Look at Balaam's words one more time:

19 God is not a man who lies, or a son of man who changes his mind! Does He speak and then not do it, or promise and not fulfill it?

God isn't like men. He cannot lie. He cannot change His mind. Everything He speaks comes to pass and all that He promises He will fulfill.

As we read through the rest of the history of Balak and Balaam, we find Balam does eventually provide Balak with a way to weaken Israel but it isn't by getting God to change His mind. Rather it was by holding onto the promises of God. Balak tried making sacrifices to get God to change.

We find in Numbers 24:12-14 Balaam's words to Balak:

12 Balaam answered Balak, "Didn't I indeed tell your messengers whom you sent to me saying: 13 If Balak were to give me his house full of silver and gold, I could not go beyond the mouth of ADONAI, to do good or bad from my own heart? Whatever ADONAI may speak, I will speak!' 14 Now, behold, I am going back to my people. Come, let me counsel you what these people will do to your people in the latter days.

Balaam reveals within these few words the answer to Balak's problems. First, while a quick read would have us to believe Balaam was saying he could not be manipulated. A careful reading shows Balaam is not saying he would not be bribed to speak against Israel. It is clear Balaam does get bribed into telling Balak what to do. Balaam is honest that he could be bribed, but he is also truthful. He knows that no amount of silver or gold can change the words coming from the mouth of God. Balaam actually says it is not a matter of what is in his heart to do. God cannot go against His own words.

Verse 14 tells us that Balaam does counsel Balak how to bring a curse upon Israel and we find the answer in Number 25:1:

1 While Israel was staying in Shittim, the people began to have immoral sexual relations with women from Moab. 2 Then they invited the people to the sacrifices of their gods, so the people were eating, and bowing down before their gods. 3 When Israel became bound to Baal of Peor, the anger of ADONAI grew hot against Israel.

Balaam knew the only way to bring a curse upon the people of Israel was for Israel to do something God promised would bring a curse upon them. In other words, Balaam told Balak God would always fulfill His word if Balam could get the children of Israel to sin, God would be obligated, by His word to bring a curse upon Israel. Balaam knew he could not cause God to go back on His word or break His promises. Instead, He told Balak how to use the promises of God against Israel.

Notice what the book of Revelation says about Balaam in Chapter 2:14:

14 But I have a few things against you. You have some there who hold to the teaching of Balaam, who was teaching Balak to put a stumbling block before B'nei-Israel, to eat food sacrificed to idols and to commit sexual immorality.

Balaam taught Balak how to bring God's promised judgment upon Israel. Remember God promised Israel both blessings and curses.

We find the choice between blessings and curses throughout the Commandments in Exodus and Leviticus, but we find it most succinctly in Deuteronomy 11:26-28:

26 See, I am setting before you today a blessing and a curse— 27 the blessing, if you listen to the mitzvot of ADONAI your God that I am commanding you today, 28 but the curse, if you do not listen to the mitzvot of ADONAI your God, but turn from the way I am commanding you today, to go after other gods you have not known.

And once again, we read of our choice of blessing or curse in the end time prophetic words which are coming to pass in front of our eyes today in Deuteronomy 30:1-10:

1 Now when all these things come upon you—the blessing and the curse that I have set before you—and you take them to heart in all the nations where ADONAI your God has banished you, 2 and you return to ADONAI your God and listen to His voice according to all that I am commanding you today—you and your children—with all your heart and with all your soul, 3 then ADONAI your God will bring you back from captivity and have compassion on you, and He will return and gather you from all the peoples where ADONAI your God has scattered you. 4 Even if your outcasts are at the ends of the heavens, from there ADONAI your God will gather you, and from there He will bring you. 5 ADONAI your God will bring you into the land that your fathers possessed, and you will possess it; and He will do you good and multiply you more than your fathers. 6 Also ADONAI your God will circumcise your heart and the heart of your descendants—to love ADONAI your God with all your heart and with all your soul, in order that you may live. 7 ADONAI your God will put all these curses on your enemies and on those who hate you, who persecuted you. 8 Then you—you will return and listen to the voice of ADONAI and do all His mitzvot that I am commanding you today. 9 ADONAI your God will make you prosper in all the work of your hand—in the fruit of your womb, and the offspring of your livestock, and the produce of your soil—for good. For ADONAI will again rejoice over you for good, as He rejoiced over your fathers— 10 when you listen to the voice of ADONAI your God, to keep His mitzvot and His statutes that are written in this scroll of the Torah, when you turn to ADONAI your God with all your heart and with all your soul.

We will look into the keeping of Mitzvot (commandments) and their influence on our receiving the promises of God further in this book. But for now, the portions of text I would like to focus in here is in verse 1 and 2. Pointing out the connection between the blessing and the curse, which we can only fully understand when we take to our heart the "His voice" or stated another way His word or promises.

For reference purposes, I want to point out two opposing examples of understanding the promises of God. The first is Balaam, of whom we just read and the second is the example of Peter and John in Acts Chapter 3. Both events show a complete confidence in God keeping His promises. In the book of Numbers, we read Balaam knew God would keep His word and bring a curse upon Israel if Israel would enter into idolatry. Balaam used sexual immorality to lead the Israelites into idolatry.

In the book of Acts chapter 3:1-7:

1 Now Peter and John were going up to the Temple at the ninth hour, the time of prayer. 2 A man lame from birth was being carried—every day they used to put him at the Temple gate called Beautiful, so he could beg for tzedakah from those entering the Temple. 3 When he saw Peter and John about to go into the Temple, he began asking to receive tzedakah. 4 But Peter, along with John, looked straight at him and said, "Look at us! 5 So he gave them his attention, expecting to receive something from them. 6 But Peter said, "Silver and gold I do not have, but what I do have I give to you—in the name of Yeshua ha-Mashiach ha-

Natzrati, get up and walk! 7 Then grabbing him by the right hand, he raised him up; and immediately the man's feet and ankles were made strong.

The contrast between these two events is not often connected but let's look at it for a moment. In Balaam's case, he takes silver and gold riches to bring a promise of God upon the children of Israel. In the case of Peter and John they bring a promise upon a child of Israel while stating they have no silver or gold. Neither, the blessing or the curse came as a result of silver or gold. Both came because the ones speaking understood the un-changeable, uncompromising eternal promises of God. Both Peter and John and Balaam new with assurance God would do exactly what He said He would do. Their motives were different. Peter and John wanted to give and bless; Balaam wanted to curse and take. But both knew without a shadow of doubt everything was as Balaam said:

I could not go beyond the mouth of ADONAI, to do good or bad from my own heart?

Earlier in this section I made mention of the similarities between the words of Balak spoken to Balaam and the words God had spoken to Abraham. This thread of connection using those words is not arbitrary. They hold a clear connection to each other and to the understanding of the promises of God to His people.

The Book of Hebrews brings into focus this connection between Balaam and Abraham again when we read the words in Hebrews chapter 6:13-18:

13 Now when God made His promise to Abraham— since He could swear by no one greater, He swore by Himself, 14 saying, "Surely I will bless you, and surely I will multiply you. 15 And so after waiting patiently, Abraham reached the promise. 16 For people swear by someone greater; and the oath, as confirmation, is an end to all their disputing. 17 In the same way God, determining to point out more clearly to the heirs of the promise the unchanging nature of His purpose, guaranteed it with an oath. 18 So by two unchangeable things, in which it is impossible for God to lie, we who have fled for refuge might have strong encouragement to take hold of the hope set before us.

Notice the repetition of the two concepts: God's promises, and God's inability to lie.

Now that we have built a foundation based upon the truth that God cannot lie, we can begin to explore the pattern found in a conversation that lasted only a few minutes but is still speaking to us over 2000 years later. This pattern exists in five parts, which we find in the words, and events that take place in those few minutes.

Let's briefly review. The criminal recognizes Yeshua as Messiah and asks Yeshua, "Remember me when You come into Your Kingdom" (The Acceptance). Yeshua then responds, "Amen I tell you, today you shall me with Me in Paradise" (The Promise received). The next thing that happens to the criminal after such an amazing promise is his legs are broken (The Breaking). The breaking is then followed by the criminal dying (The Death). After the criminal dies, he is in Paradise with Yeshua (The Promise Fulfilled). The five parts of the pattern are (1) The Acceptance, (2) The Promise Received, (3) The Breaking, (4) The Death (5) The Promise Fulfilled.

In order to discuss this pattern and see if it holds true throughout the Bible, let's survey the lives of seven Biblical characters: Adam, Abraham, Jacob, Joseph, Moses, Samson and Peter.

I am limiting the study to seven, not because the pattern is limited, but it is my desire for many people to read this book and learn to apply the pattern to their lives.

Irrevocable Patterns of Promise Questions

1) Name three irrevocable promise patterns:

2) Can you name a promise pattern God has kept in your life?

3) Can you name a promise pattern God kept in someone else's life?

4) Can you name a promise pattern you are still waiting to be kept?

5) What promise pattern would you like to see fulfilled in your life?

Acceptance

The first part of the five-part pattern is the acceptance. In the narrative we are studying. The acceptance is found in the following statements within the verses.

"Don't you fear God, since you are under the same sentence? We're getting what we deserve for our actions, and rightly so—but this One has done nothing wrong."

It was with great surprise he realized that those words had come out of his own mouth. He continued speaking with complete faith saying,

"Yeshua, remember me when You come into Your kingdom."

We notice right away the criminal knew Yeshua was innocent of the accusations of which he was tried and condemned. But the real key to knowing this man recognized and accepted Yeshua as Messiah, is in the second statement above.

The proof comes in two parts. The first is found in his use of the name Yeshua. Remember names have meanings and the name Yeshua means salvation.

Matthew 1:21:

21 She will give birth to a son; and you shall call His name Yeshua, for He will save His people from their sins."

When we read the entire interaction between the two criminals and Yeshua notice the criminal who rejects Yeshua uses the pronoun "he" as he mocks the term "Messiah." While the other identifies with his recognition of who Yeshua is with his mention of salvation. But further proof of acceptance is found in the use of the words "Your kingdom" that is even clearer proof of the acceptance as the Messiah Son of David would be the One who would establish the messianic kingdom described in the Scriptures.

There is be no doubt that this man accepted Yeshua as the Messiah of Israel and as a result of that acceptance, became eligible to receive all of the promises given by God to those who are part of His covenants.

So we see the first step in the pattern to receive and walk within the promised blessings of God is established. One must demonstrate true acceptance of Yeshua as the Messiah.

Many books have been written on how to accept Him and be born again. If you are not a born again believer in Yeshua, I encourage you to stop reading this book and begin to read the Bible until you are convinced He is in fact, the Messiah who came to bring forgiveness from sins and a new life. I suggest you begin reading in the Book of John especially reading all of Chapter 3.

Once you have come to accept Yeshua and achieved part one, continue reading to learn how to walk in the blessings promised to a believer.

The acceptance of God is shown first by Adam and Eve in Genesis chapter 3:3-5:

But of the fruit of the tree which is in the middle of the garden, God said, 'You must not eat of it and you must not touch it, or you will die.' 4 The serpent said to the woman, "You most assuredly won't die! 5 For God knows that when you eat of it, your eyes will be opened and you will be like God, knowing good and evil.

I know the conversation we read in this text is between Eve and the serpent. However we note, while Eve is the one talking, it is clear from the text that Adam is with her during this conversation. Eve proclaims God said they shall not eat of the fruit of the tree in the middle of the garden. It is clear from the statement that although they ultimately do eat of the fruit, they also previously recognized God was God. This recognition demonstrates Adam and Eve's acceptance of God.

Abraham

Abraham's acceptance of God is found in Genesis 12:1-4:

1 Then ADONAI said to Abram, "Get going out from your land, and from your relatives, and from your father's house, to the land that I will show you. 2 My heart's desire is to make you into a great nation, to bless you, to make your name great so that you may be a blessing. 3 I will bless those who bless you, but whoever curses you I will curse, and in you all the families of the earth will be blessed. 4 So Abram went, just as ADONAI had spoken to him. Also Lot went with him. (Now Abram was 75 years old when he departed from Haran.)

Abraham hears God's voice calling him and responds to the call by doing just what God had spoken to him. Abraham doesn't just hear what God says to him and continue to do what he was doing before, rather he immediately obeys God's instructions. Abraham's obedience to God demonstrates his acceptance of Adonai as God.

In Genesis 28 Jacob has a unique experience which brings him to a place of accepting God. Jacob left his father house in a hurry because of his deception against his father Isaac and brother Esau. He is on his way to his uncle's house at the direction of both his mother and father and along the way he meets God for himself. Previous to this time he knew God not as his God but as the God of his father. We read in Genesis 27:

20 Then Isaac said to his son, "How in the world were you able to find it so quickly, my son?" He said, "Because ADONAI your God made it happen for me.

We can see in the text that as Jacob is lying to his father he does so in part because he knew God as his father's God and not as his own God. It isn't until after he runs away and has the dream of the ladder to heaven, that he acknowledges God is present in Genesis 28:16-17:

16 Jacob woke up from his sleep and said, "Undoubtedly, ADONAI is in this place—and I was unaware. 17 So he was afraid and said, "How fearsome this place is! This is none other than the House of God—this must be the gate of heaven!

Jacob's acceptance of God's existence and His presence at Beth El was only a partial recognition. It was not enough Jacob just accepted God existed. Full acceptance requires a relational aspect. Found in Scripture as we continue reading in Genesis 28:18-22:

18 Early in the morning Jacob got up and took the stone, which he had placed by his head, and set it up as a memorial stone and poured oil on top of it. 19 He called the name of that place Beth-El (though originally the city's name was Luz). 20 Then Jacob made a vow saying, "If God will be with me and watch over me on this way that I am going, and provide me food to eat and clothes to wear, 21 and I return in shalom to my father's house, then ADONAI will be my God. 22 So this stone which I set up as a memorial stone will become God's House, and of everything You provide me I will definitely give a tenth of it to You.

Beginning in verse 18 we see the transition from an understanding that God exists to an understanding that God is relational and Jacob entered a relationship with him. Notice Jacob builds a place of worship and enters into a personal covenant relationship with God, not as his father Isaac's God but as his own God.

Joseph

Joseph's acceptance of God and His promises is demonstrated in his acceptance of the dreams God gave to him. His actions in immediately sharing those dreams, while possibly bad timing, clearly shows he believed the promises in the dreams and that they came directly from God. While there does not seem to be a verbal acceptance of the promises made, there is a clear response by Joseph showing he accepted those promises and immediately changed his actions to line up with his new beliefs.

For those who are believers already acceptance is step one. You have already completed that part. So please continue through the balance of the remaining four steps.

For those who have not yet accepted that God loves you so much that He provided the Bible as a record of expressing that love to you, know that every word contained was written, in order to provide instructions to lead you to faith in Yeshua, who was God became flesh dwelling amoung us.

John 1:14 And the Word became flesh and tabernacled among us. We looked upon His glory, the glory of the one and only from the Father, full of grace and truth.

In coming in the flesh, Yeshua lived a perfect life according to Torah and became the offering for our sins to pay a price that we could not possible pay.

Isaiah 53:10 Yet it pleased Adonai to bruise Him. He caused Him to suffer. If He makes His soul a guilt offering, He will see His offspring, He will prolong His days, and the will of Adonai will succeed by His hand.

It is my hope that before you reach the end of this book, you will have accepted God as your Creator and Father and Yeshua as your Messiah and Redeemer.

The remaining parts of the pattern will be covered in the next four sections of this book, as we review the lives of Biblical characters as they progress from *Promise Received to Promise Fulfilled.*

Moses

Moses is tending sheep in Midian when God calls to him from within a burning bush. We find Moses' calling in Exodus 3:4-6:

4 When Adonai saw that he turned to look, He called to him out of the midst of the bush and said, "Moses, Moses!" So he answered, "Hineni." 5 Then He said, "Come no closer. Take your sandals off your feet, for the place where you are standing is holy ground." 6 Moreover He said, "I am the God of your father, the God of Abraham, Isaac and Jacob." So Moses hid his face, because he was afraid to look at God.

Notice that in these verses we have God speaking to Moses and Moses accepting He is God proven by his four actions in response to God's calling. First, when hiding himself in fear so as not to look upon God. Second, Moses shows acceptance of God when he asks Jethro to let him return to Egypt in Chapter 4:18:

18So Moses went, returned to his father-in-law Jethro and said to him, "Please let me go, so I may return to my kinsmen who are in Egypt and see whether they are still alive." Jethro said to Moses, "Go in peace."

Thirdly, in Chapter 4:20 we see Moses taking the staff of God in his hand.

20 So Moses took his wife and his sons, set them on a donkey and returned to the land of Egypt. Moses took the staff of God in his hand.

Fourth, we find Tzipporah, Moses' wife, in anger performing circumcision on her son in response to what would be Moses' desire to have them enter the covenant of Abraham. Her anger had to be in response to Moses accepting God as his God and then wanting his sons to enter into His covenant. These four actions clearly show Moses' acceptance of God as his God.

Samson

Samson's acceptance is different from characters we've studied thus far as each have a written dialogue between themselves and God which documents a calling and a response or acceptance of God. Samson's call does not show a direct calling and acceptance because the text of Scripture does not provide for us a record of the conversation. What Scripture does provide is a record of the conversation between God and Samson's parents this is followed up by statements that speak of Samson being stirred by the Spirit of God such as in Judges Chapter 13:24 and 14:6. The verses show an implied acceptance because of the activity of the Spirit of God in the life of Samson. Notice in the text below, Samson grew up and God blessed him and began to stir within him.

24 Then the woman bore a son, and called his name Samson. So the boy grew up and Adonai blessed him.

25The Ruach Adonai began to stir him in Mahaneh-dan, between Zorah and Eshtaol.

6Then the Ruach Adonai came mightily upon him, and he tore him apart as one would have split a young goat—yet he had nothing in his hand. But he did not tell his father or his mother what he had done.

We know from Scripture that God does not force people to accept the moving of the Spirit. The simple truth is the Spirit moving within Samson confirms Samson accepted God as his God.

Peter

We find the calling of Peter and his acceptance in the records of Matthew 4 and Luke 5. Starting with the account in the book of Luke, we find the longest account of Peters acceptance. It must have seemed happenstance when Yeshua walked over and stood next to Peter's boat. Then to make the event even more unusual, Yeshua stepped into the boat and instructed Peter to push away into deep water and cast his nets. This was unique, especially since Peter and his crew were busy cleaning the nets after a long night of fishing. Yet Peter, out of respect was willing to obey, and, as a result of his willingness to do the illogical, the nets were filled with fish unto overflowing. Peter's response was to immediately confess his fallen nature as a sinful man. Yeshua's reply was the same as it is to our similar confessions today, "don't be afraid." Peter, according to Matthew 4:18-20, immediately walked away from his nets and boat and began to follow Yeshua.

Luke 5:1 It happened that the crowds were pressing upon Yeshua to hear the word of God as He was standing by the Lake of Kinneret, 2 when He saw two boats standing beside the lake. Now the fishermen had left them and were washing the nets. 3 Getting into one of the boats, Simon's boat, Yeshua asked him to push out a way from the land. Then sitting down, He taught the crowds from the boat. 4 When He had finished speaking, He said to Simon, "Go out into the deep water, and let down your nets for a catch." 5 Simon replied, "Master, we've worked hard all night and caught nothing. But at Your word I will let down the nets." *6 When they had done this, they caught so many fish that their nets began to break.7 So they signaled to their partners in the other boat to come and help them. They came and filled both boats so full that they began to sink. 8 But when Simon Peter saw this, he fell down at Yeshua's knees, saying, "Go away from me, Master, for I am a sinful man!" 9 For amazement had gripped him and all who were with him, over the catch of fish they had netted; 10 so also Jacob and John, Zebedee's sons, who were partners with Simon. But Yeshua said to Simon, "Do not be afraid. From now on, you will be catching men." 11So when they had brought the boats to the landing, they left everything and followed Him.*

Matthew 4:18 Now as Yeshua was walking by the Sea of Galilee, He saw two brothers, Simon who was called Peter and Andrew his brother. They were casting a net into the sea, for they were fishermen.19 And He said to them, "Follow Me, and I will make you fishers of men."20 Immediately they left their nets and followed Him.

Eric

In my life, I can remember when I was a child attending synagogue services and Hebrew school listening to the story and history of my people. Bored out of my skull and hoping something exciting would happen like the sanctuary roof collapsing or the teacher's chair breaking, dumping her noisily onto the floor. I heard the prayers and read the portions of Scripture assigned each week and sang the liturgy along with the rest of the congregation. However, the highlight of my synagogue experience each Shabbat was the sudden crashing sound caused by birds flying into the windows lining the sanctuary ceiling.

My family was active in our synagogue, which meant we went to Friday evening service and Saturday morning services and I attended Hebrew School twice during the week and on Shabbat morning. When asked why this was so important, especially since attending these services and classes meant I would not be able to join my friends in afternoon ball games. It also meant I always missed Saturday morning cartoons on television. My parent's answer to my pleading was simply, we went to synagogue because we were Jews. I was a Jew. To me that meant I was to suffer through nearly intolerable dry, meaningless services and spend five hours a week studying about being a Jew. We are a chosen people, I was told. Chosen for what? Chosen to suffer death by boredom, a slow painful demise caused by slowing dripping totally unimportant information onto my head in droning monotone lessons.

This all changed dramatically in 1973, when as an 11 year old boy I listened to the news reports about the Yom Kippur war. Israel's victory, in some way, dragged the God of the Bible into my world and I became a believer. The only explanation for Israel winning this war, when the enemy was so much larger and better armed, was that the same God who protected Israel in the Bible was protecting Israel outside of the Bible. My life changed that day. I began to pray, not just reciting ancient prayers that were passed down from generation to generation. But I began to believe if God was still active today protecting his people and I was one of His people, then my prayers, spoken from my heart would be heard by that very same God. That day was not the first time that God called me, but it was the first time I listened and responded to His call.

The criminal on the cross heard the words, "Father forgive them" and brought recognition that there was a God. For me, I heard the news reports announcing victory for a small nation, surround by larger better equipped, armies and I knew there was a God.

The Acceptance Questions

1) Do you remember the moment you accepted God exists?

2) What Changed?

3) What new questions did this acceptance bring?

4) What didn't change?

5) Did you tell anyone when you accepted the existence of God?

The Promise

Take a look at Luke 23:43:

"Amen, I tell you, today you shall be with Me in Paradise."

In this section we will look only into the various promises God gave to our seven characters in our survey. We will cover what their promises were and their response to their promise.

As is often said the best place to start looking at the promises of God is with the very first promises made to mankind vocally. When studying the Scriptures, we must always remember the only way one can truly understand a biblical concept is by starting at the very first reference. Taking a closer look at promises made to man, appropriately the first promise we should start with is the Adam. Genesis 2:16-17:

16 Then ADONAI Elohim commanded the man saying,

"From all the trees of the garden you are most welcome to eat. 17 But of the Tree of the Knowledge of Good and Evil you must not eat. For when you eat from it, you most assuredly will die!

When we look at this very first promise God spoke to the very first man whom he formed with his very own hands from the ground, we notice it was not a promise of blessing, but rather a promise of death. Why one may ask? Simply because God placed Adam in a garden, a state of permanent blessing. In the garden of Eden there was no sickness, no pain, even the gardens Adam was assigned to tend had no weeds. Even better, Adam was created by God without any understanding of evil or sin.

He lived in a reality of complete love and blessings. Just imagine a world like that where you could live forever and ever.

Adam

Adam's first promise from God was simply, if you eat of the

fruit of the Tree of Knowledge of Good and Evil you will die. Adam had no way to personally relate to the concept of death because no one had ever died. His concept of death was equivalent to Noah's concept of rain in a world where it had never rained. Both Adam and Noah had to accept a promise spoken by God that included within it a fulfillment that was beyond their personal understanding or experience. Which immediately brings to mind a definition of faith that we find in Hebrews 11:1:

1 Now faith is the substance of things hoped for, the evidence of realities not seen.

The second promise made to mankind was not spoken to Adam but to Adam and Eve: Genesis 3:15:

15 I will put animosity between you and the woman— between your seed and her seed. He will crush your head, and you will crush his heel.

Notice this promise was made as a result of Adam and Eve not trusting God, which caused Him to be faithful to the promise. Adam and Eve would now die physically, but even knowing how tragic this punishment for Adam and Eve's failure to trust God, God still did not give up on Adam and Eve. Instead, He provided another promise. This promise was one of victory over the adversary.

Abraham

While we can see many promises between Adam and Abraham, for the purposes of this book we are going to jump from the very first man to the very first Hebrew, Abraham. Because there is a direct correlation between the redemptive promise made to Adam and Eve after their fall and the promise given to Abraham at his calling by God and it is by this promise or covenant all, both Jewish and non-Jewish, have access to eternal life. As we follow the thread of promise from Adam, the father of all mankind, to Abraham, the Father of the nation Israel, we should immediately connect the promise of the "seed of Adam" crushing the head of the adversary with the promise that the "seed of Abraham" would bring blessings to all people.

We read in Genesis 12:1-3:

1 Then ADONAI said to Abram, "Get going out from your land, and from your relatives, and from your father's house, to the land that I will show you. 2 My heart's desire is to make you into a great nation, to bless you, to make your name great so that you may be a blessing. 3 I will bless those who bless you, but whoever curses you I will curse, and in you all the families of the earth will be blessed.

It is through this singular promise all the families of the earth would be blessed in Abraham. This promise is explained further in Galatians 3:28-29, through Yeshua, who was from the seed of Abraham, the fullness of this promise is provided and:

28 There is neither Jew nor Greek, there is neither slave nor free, there is neither male nor female—for you are all one in Messiah Yeshua. 29 And if you belong to Messiah, then you are Abraham's seed—heirs according to the promise.

God has called Abraham to leave his land, relatives and father's house and go to a land God would show him. The promise continues that Abraham who was childless and 75 years old at the time would become a great nation. As we look deeper into the promise and the response to the promise, we find Abraham was told not just to leave his father's house but also to leave his relatives. However, we know Abraham did not follow God's instructions to the letter. We continue reading on with Genesis 12:4-5:

4 So Abram went, just as ADONAI had spoken to him. Also Lot went with him. (Now Abram was 75 years old when he departed from Haran.) 5 Abram took Sarai his wife, and Lot his nephew, and all their possessions that they had acquired, and the people that they acquired in Haran, and they left to go to the land of Canaan, and they entered the land of Canaan.

Notice that although Abraham did pack up his things and leave heading to the Land of Promise, he also brought Lot his nephew along with him. Abraham had received a promise and believed enough to begin a journey to a place he not only had never been, but also without having any idea where he was going. That's faith, but as with many of us, we may have faith to follow

God but, we have some limits to our great faith. In Abraham's case he was willing to do everything except leave his relatives behind in Haran.

It is possible that Yeshua's comments in Mark 10:29:

29 Amen, I tell you," Yeshua replied, "there is no one who has left house or brothers or sisters or mother or father or children or property, for My sake and for the sake of the Good News, 30 who will not receive a hundred times as much now in this time, houses and brothers and sisters and mothers and children and property, along with persecutions; and in the olam ha-ba, eternal life.

It's a reminder that we must be willing to give up all like Abraham as we make our journey to the eternal Promised Land. It is important for us to make note of as we continue to read Genesis 12:7:

7 Then ADONAI appeared to Abram, and said, "I will give this land to your seed." So there he built an altar to ADONAI, who had appeared to him.

Even though Abraham did not completely obey God when he brought Lot with him, God did not give up on Abraham or break His promise. Instead, God took the time to reconfirm his promise to Abraham. Abraham's immediate response to this reconfirmation of promise was to worship God.

In Genesis 12: 1-3 God not only promised Abraham the Land of Canaan which would later become Israel, He also promised he would make him a "Great Nation." In other words, he would have many children. In Genesis 15:5 we read the continuation of this promise:

1 After these things the word of ADONAI came to Abram in a vision saying, "Do not fear, Abram. I am your shield, your very great reward. 2 But Abram said, "My Lord ADONAI, what will You give me, since I am living without children, and the heir of my household is Eliezer of Damascus? 3 Then Abram said, "Look! You have given me no seed, so a house-born servant is my heir. 4 Then behold, the word of ADONAI came to him saying, "This one will not be your heir, but in fact, one who will come from your own body will be your heir. 5 He took him outside and said, "Look up now, at the sky, and count the stars—if you are able to count them." Then He said to him, "So shall your seed be."

In these verses we read God reiterates his promise by telling Abraham, who at the time is still without any children, his seed would be as many as the stars in the sky. This promise is then once again made to Abraham in Genesis 22:17-18 after he demonstrates his trust in God's sovereignty by being willing to sacrifice Isaac:

17 I will richly bless you and bountifully multiply your seed like the stars of heaven, and like the sand that is on the seashore, and your seed will possess the gate of his enemies. 18 In your seed all the nations of the earth will be blessed —because you obeyed My voice.

Abraham does eventually have children. He and his wife Sarah have Isaac and after Sarah's death, Abraham married Keturah and had six more children. But according to the Scriptures, Abraham understood Isaac was the child of promise and the son in which God's promise of God to Abraham was to continue. In Genesis 25:5:

5 Now Abraham gave everything that he had to Isaac.

We also read where God speaks to Isaac in Genesis 26:2-5: **2 Then ADONAI appeared to him and said, "Do not go down to Egypt. Dwell in the land about which I tell you. 3 Live as an outsider in this land and I will be with you and bless you—for to you and to your seed I give all these lands—and I will confirm my pledge that I swore to Abraham your father. 4 I will multiply your seed like the stars of the sky and I will give your seed all these lands. And in your seed all the nations of the earth will continually be blessed, 5 because Abraham listened to My voice and kept My charge, My mitzvot, My decrees, and My instructions.**

In these verses we see the continuation of God's promise to Abraham passed on to Isaac and his descendants. This promise is still in effect today as God is still blessing the nations through the "Seed of Abraham" which ultimately was a reference to Yeshua who brought redemption and salvation to the whole world.

Just as Abraham had several promises given to him: the promise of the land, the promise of having a great name, blessings of those who blessed him and curse on him who curse him and that all the families of the earth would be blessed by him. Isaac also received more than one promise. Looking at Isaac's promises in the verses above we see that God promises to always be with Isaac, to bless him, to give him the land, and all the nations would be not just blessed, but continually blessed. Many of these promises are not specifically for Abraham and Isaac but are passed on from generation to generation as the nation fathered by Abraham continues. Each promise or covenant provided by God to man is built upon the foundation of each previous covenant or promise as confirmed not only in the Old Testament but this truth is reiterated in the New Testament, in the book of Galatians chapter 3:15:18:

15 Brethren, I speak in human terms: even with a man's covenant, once it has been confirmed, no one cancels it or adds to it. 16 Now the promises were spoken to Abraham and to his seed. It doesn't say, "and to seeds," as of many, but as of one, "and to your seed," who is the Messiah. 17 What I am saying is this: Torah, which came 430 years later, does not cancel the covenant previously confirmed by God, so as to make the promise ineffective. 18 For if the inheritance is based on law, it is no longer based on a promise. But God has graciously given it to Abraham by means of a promise.

This series of verses is directly connected to the promises given to Abraham and confirmed to Isaac and applies to all those who would become the "seed" of Abraham through the "Seed of Promise", Yeshua.

Jacob

We know the birthright or linage promise continued from Abraham to Isaac and then to Jacob. This passing from Isaac to Jacob was also based on a promise given by God to Rebekah in Genesis 25:22-23:

22 But the children struggled with one another inside her, and she said, "If it's like this, why is this happening to me?" So she went to inquire of ADONAI.

23 ADONAI said to her: "Two nations are in your womb, and two peoples from your body will be separated. One people will be stronger than the other people, but the older will serve the younger.

24 When her time came to give birth, indeed there were twins in her womb.

Without going through all of the interactions and deceptions that took place between Isaac, Rebekah, Esau and Jacob due to their failures to trust in God's promises, let's continue with the generational covenant promise spoken to Jacob as he is running for his life from his older brother Esau. Jacob stops for the night on his journey and has a dream in which he dreamed of a stairway reaching to the heavens with angels of God going up and down.

In this dream, at the lowest point of spirituality in Jacob's life, we find Jacob is being chased by his brother after he has conspired with his mother, lied to his father and stolen from his brother blessings, God gives to Jacob the following promises. In Genesis 28:13-15:

13 Surprisingly, ADONAI was standing on top of it and He said, "I am ADONAI, the God of your father Abraham and the God of Isaac. The land on which you lie, I will give it to you and to your seed. 14 Your seed will be as the dust of the land, and you will burst forth to the west and to the east and to the north and to the south. And in you all the families of the earth will be blessed—and in your seed.

15 Behold, I am with you, and I will watch over you wherever you go, and I will bring you back to this land, for I will not forsake you until I have done what I promised you.

Jacob's promises contain not just the promised rights to the Land given first to his grandfather Abraham, and the continuing "seed promise" which was given to Adam, but the addition of four promises given just to Jacob. The promise of God's continued presence in his life and wherever he travels. The promise God would watch over him all the while protecting him. The promise that God would bring him back to the covenant land. The promise God would never forsake him. Once again, it is important to point out this visitation in a dream by God to Jacob, in which God gave Jacob these awesome promises took place not when Jacob was at a spiritual high point in his life, but at a time when he had sinned greatly. He was running away, not just from Esau who wanted to kill him, but also from the very blessings of covenant promises he and Rebekah had deceived his father and brother to steal. Think about it. While he was running as fast and as far as he could away from the promises of God, God showed up and reminded him of the very promises he was running away from. God didn't stop at reminding him of the promises that were his by inheritance or birthright. God, at the moment in Jacob's life when we would assume that God would be most disappointed with Jacob because of his sin, He demonstrates, once again, He will keep His promises.

Joseph

From Jacob's promises we continue our study to Joseph, Jacob's first born son with Rachael. Joseph's promise came as his father Jacob's also came, in the form of dreams.

Genesis 37:5 *Then Joseph dreamed a dream and told his brothers—and they hated him even more. 6 He said to them, "Please listen to this dream I dreamed. 7 There we were binding sheaves in the middle of the field. All of a sudden, my sheaf arose and stood upright. And behold, your sheaves gathered around and bowed down to my sheaf. 8 Will you truly be a king over us?" his brothers said to him. "Will you really rule over us?" So they hated him even more because of his dreams and because of his words. 9 But then he dreamed another dream and told it to his brothers, saying, "I have just dreamed another dream. Suddenly, there was the sun and the moon and the eleven stars bowing down to me! 10 He told it to his father as well as his brothers. Then his father rebuked him and said to him, "What's this dream you dreamed? Will we really come—your mother and I with your brothers—to bow down to the ground to you? 11 So his brothers were jealous of him, but his father kept the speech in mind.*

Joseph's promise showed he would rise to a place of authority, not only over his brothers, but also his father. Although Joseph is not the son who carried on the birthright covenant, he is considered to be one of the most powerful

100

symbolic forerunners of Yeshua. Within the events of Joseph's life, we see so many types and shadows in the life of Joseph that precursor Yeshua.

Just a few to consider.

- He was rejected by his brothers as Yeshua was at His first coming. But later was revealed as the one who years later when his brothers were looking for a means of salvation revealed himself and provided salvation for his brothers.
- Joseph was sold for a price and Yeshua was sold for a price.
- Joseph falsely accused of a crime, Yeshua was falsely accused.
- Joseph was about 30 years old when he went to the King of Egypt to provide salvation for the whole world. Yeshua was about 30 when he went to The Father and provided salvation for the whole world. The promise given in Joseph's dream not only told of the means of the temporary salvation of Israel, but foretold the permanent salvation of Israel. These are only a few of the many ways Joseph's life mirrors Yeshua's life. Each of these similarities are a part of

the promise of Joseph that goes far beyond the initial fulfillment that took place within the lifetime of Joseph.

Moses

We find Moses' promise in Exodus chapter 3:10 while he is tending sheep in the wilderness around Midian and he came upon a bush that is on fire but not being consumed. From the bush comes the promise God makes to Moses. It is contained in one simple statement.

10 Come now, I will send you to Pharaoh, so that you may bring My people Bnei-Yisrael out from Egypt.

God introduced Himself to Moses as the God of Abraham, Isaac and Jacob with a clear purpose in mind. Although Moses was known as a child of Pharaoh's daughter, he was raised by his actual mother who provided him with a knowledge of his history as a Hebrew and because of that he knew the God of Israel is a God of promises.

Promises not only made but kept. In one small sentence God not only promises Moses He was going to use him to deliver the Children of Israel from slavery.

Those few words also provided a clear word of encouragement designed to give Moses confidence in God's promises based upon the proven history of God's faithfulness to His promises. The power of the phrase "My People" being used rather than "Your People" is a reminder not just to Moses but to us today that God always keeps His promises.

Samson

Although we could go through every promise God ever spoke to a human being, for the sake of brevity, we are going to cover two more examples, one from the Tanakh, Samson and one from the New Covenant, Peter.

Samson's promise is different so far in that it was actually made not to him directly but to his parents in Judges 13:1-5:

1 Bnei-Yisrael again did what was evil in in ADONAI's eyes, and ADONAI gave them into the hand of the Philistines for 40 years. 2 Now there was a certain man from Zorah, from a Danite clan, whose name was Manoah. His wife was barren and bore no children. 3 Then the angel of ADONAI appeared to the woman and said to her, "Behold now, you are barren and have not borne children, but you will conceive and bear a son. 4 Now therefore be careful not to drink wine or strong drink, or eat any unclean thing. 5 For behold, you will conceive and bear a son. Let no razor come upon his head, for the boy will be a Nazirite to God from the womb. He will begin to deliver Israel from the hand of the Philistines.

Samson's promise also came with parental requirements. His mother was instructed to not eat any unclean thing and to abstain from wine and strong drink. Samson was to live the life of one who has taken a Nazarite vow. The Nazarite vow is explained in Number 6:1-8:

1 Again ADONAI spoke to Moses saying, 2 Speak to Bnei-Yisrael and say to them: Any man or woman who desires to vow a Nazirite vow to be separate for ADONAI, 3 is to abstain from wine and any other fermented drink. He is not to drink any vinegar made from wine or any fermented drink, or any grape juice, or eat grapes or raisins. 4 All during his days as a Nazirite he is not to eat anything from the grapevine— even the seeds or skins. 5 All the duration of his Nazirite vow, no razor is to come on his head until the time of his consecration to ADONAI is over. He is to be holy, and the hair of his head is to grow long. 6 All the days of his separation to ADONAI, he is not to go near a dead body. 7 Even if his father, mother, brother or sister should die, he is not to make himself unclean, because his consecration to God is on his head. 8 All the days of his separation, he is to be consecrated to ADONAI.

Samson's promise was that God was going to use him to begin to deliver Israel from the Philistines.

Peter

In the case of Peter, we are going to look at not one but two promises spoken to him by Yeshua. The first is in Mathew chapter 16:13-19:

13 When Yeshua came into the region of Caesarea Philippi, He asked His disciples, "Who do people say that the Son of Man is? 14 They answered, "Some say John the Immerser, others say Elijah, and still others say Jeremiah or one of the other prophets. 15 He said, "But who do you say I am? 16 Simon Peter answered, "You are the Messiah, the Son of the living God. 17 Yeshua said to him, "Blessed are you, Simon son of Jonah, because flesh and blood did not reveal this to you, but My Father who is in heaven! 18 And I also tell you that you are Peter, and upon this rock I will build My community; and the gates of Sheol will not overpower it. 19 I will give you the keys of the kingdom of heaven. Whatever you forbid on earth will have been forbidden in heaven and what you permit on earth will have been permitted in heaven.

The second is found in Luke 22:31-34:

31 Simon, Simon! Indeed, Satan has demanded to sift

you all like wheat. 32 But I have prayed for you, Simon, that your faith will not fail. And when you have turned back, strengthen your brethren." 33 But Simon said to Him, "Master, I am ready to go with You even to prison and to death!" 34 But Yeshua said, "I tell you, Peter, a rooster will not crow today until you have denied three times that you know Me.

These two sections of verses are well known by most believers and show three different but related promises given to Peter. The verses in Mathew 16 show Yeshua promising Peter he was to receive the "Keys to the Kingdom."

The second promise is different yet intimately connects. It contains two parts and if we read the verses correctly, Yeshua is telling Peter He has prayed for him because He knows Peter is going to fall. We know this because of the wording, "And when you have turned back." Other Bibles used the word when you have repented, which is what turning back means. The point being, Yeshua's promise was that Peter was going to fall and then turn back. The second part of the promise actually tells Peter exactly how he was going to fall; he would deny Yeshua three time in the very same day that Yeshua gave Peter the promise.

Eric

I remember hearing a clear voice in my heart speaking with kindness, yet with an assurance and boldness that I knew it was God speaking to me. I was 19 years old and I had grown from being a child, who accepted the existence of God through turbulent years of seemingly unanswerable questions. I never began to question if there was a God. But I did question everything about Him.

My life was filled with what I considered major disasters. My parents separated and then divorced when I was around five. At seven, my father passed away from Hodgkins disease. After my father died a few years passed and my mother married my stepfather. I had moved out of my parent's home into my grandparent's house and then moved from one city to another.
My stepfather brought along with him two step brothers and two step sisters. Everything about my world was changing

too quickly and as a preteen and teenager it was impossible to tell the good from the bad. My grandparents moved out when my stepfather moved in. Along with my new family came also the influence of a new religion.

My stepfather converted to Judaism but my new siblings remained Roman Catholic. So as they unpacked along with their clothes, toys and furniture came Jesus.

This dramatic reformation of all things in my life also came while I was studying to become Bar Mitzvah. Up until this time my education consisted of learning about Judaism. I learned about Jewish History from Abraham to the Holocaust and on to modern Israel. I also learned prayers and stories from the sacred texts of my people. But I had never truly studied the actual Scriptures themselves. I listened to them in Hebrew each week as the Torah and Haf-Torah were so beautifully canted. But what those Hebrew words so skillfully sung meant was beyond my level of understanding Hebrew. For the first time I was studying the actual words in order to prepare a speech I would give during my Bar Mitzvah. It was while studying those words in English, I had my greatest crisis of faith.

Until then, my faith in God was based upon my understanding of God's covenant promises to Israel.

It was because of these promises I believed God helped Israel defeat all of the nations that attacked her in 1973. To me, the proof God was God was because He was faithful to keep His covenant promises.

However, once I started to read the Torah for myself, I was not questioning God but questioning the Jewish people. God had continued to be faithful and loving throughout history but the Jewish people clearly had not kept their side of the covenant.

The more I read, the angrier and disappointed I became in my people. I questioned everything I thought I knew about God.

Then one afternoon, while serving in the Navy, I was approached by another sailor and he asked me about my faith. He was not offensive or aggressive in his approach, Instead he was sincere and curious about my Jewish faith.

Everything was fine until he started to tell me about Jesus. It wasn't the mention of Jesus that bothered me. I had heard of him many times from my sisters and brothers. It was the way he spoke, as he described Jesus as a Jew and rabbi. This caused me to pause and think.

He was so wrong about Jesus, I thought. I knew Jesus was not a Jew, but a Catholic. He was the son of two Italians, Mary and Joseph. I went back to my barracks and began to research and the more I read the more Jewish Jesus became.

It was during this time of personal study that I received the message I spoke about earlier in this section. The Scriptures promised I was one of the Children of Israel. This promise was for me. Romans 11:25-27:

25 For I do not want you, brothers and sisters, to be ignorant of this mystery—lest you be wise in your own eyes—that a partial hardening has come upon Israel until the fullness of the Gentiles has come in; 26 and in this way all Israel will be saved, as it is written, "The Deliverer shall come out of Zion. He shall turn away ungodliness from Jacob. 27 And this is My covenant with them, when I take away their sins."

I still can hear those words today. That promise changed my life forever. It was a still, small voice speaking deep into my soul. This single promise was where I received the hope and faith to also believe my mother would come to faith in Yeshua. He came for all of Israel, including my mother and all of my family. The criminal's promise was, "Today you will be with me in Paradise." My promise was my mother would also be in Paradise.

As we look at these promises and many others given by God in the Bible, think for just a moment about how it would have felt for the recipients. Each of the promises came as the result of a supernatural encounter with God. Each promise was the result of a direct revelation and each promise was life changing.

The promises given to us in the Bible are not just to be read, they are to be received in a supernatural way. The promises of God become real to us only when we accept they were not just written in the Bible for others who lived long ago and far away, but that each and every promise is to be viewed as if God has appeared right in front of us in a burning bush or spoken audibly from the heavens. Because the truth is He has.

As you think about the promises listed in this section as well as the hundreds of other promises you are already familiar with. Take a few moments and acclimate yourself to the truth that God isn't a respecter of persons and every promise ever made to His people is for you.
Consider how the criminal felt as we read Luke 22:43:

43 Yeshua said to him, "Amen, I tell you, today you shall be with Me in Paradise.

Think about the overwhelming emotions that man must have felt when hearing those words spoken. Ask yourself, how do I react when I receive a promise from God? Do I really believe each promise given by God is not just available but promised?

The Promise Questions

1) What promise(s) have you received from God?

2) What was your response or reaction to the promise?

3) Have you shared your promise with anyone?

4) Why or why not?

5) What do you do to keep your promise fresh in your heart?

The Breaking

The breaking is found in the following statement in John 19:31-32:

31 It was the Day of Preparation, and the next day was a festival Shabbat. So that the bodies should not remain on the execution stake during Shabbat, the Judean leaders asked Pilate to have the legs broken and to have the bodies taken away.
32 So the soldiers came and broke the legs of the first and then the other who had been executed with Yeshua.

After the promise of Paradise was given to the criminal by Yeshua his legs were broken. But before his legs were broken we read in Luke 23:40-42:

40But the other one, rebuking him, replied, "Don't you fear God, since you are under the same sentence?
41We're getting what we deserve for our actions, and rightly so—but this One has done nothing wrong."

42And he said, "Yeshua, remember me when You come into Your kingdom."

The criminal had come to a place of breaking and repentance as demonstrated in his words of admission of deserving his punishment for his actions and his turning his heart to Yeshua and His kingdom.

The breaking can be described as simply as laying down our will for the will of God.

It is coming to a functional conclusion that God has already blessed us with His promises and that He doesn't need our advice or assistance in planning how to provide His promises. The breaking usually comes when situations or circumstances in our lives cause us to acknowledge our smallness in comparison to God's greatness. Breaking comes at a "Not my will but Yours be done," moment. In this section we will look at our seven Biblical characters and identify "Breaking" in their lives. We will also notice it takes more than one "Breaking" in order to achieve "The Breaking."

The Breaking is an experience in which the one who has received a promise from God and then fails or sins, is then broken by the experience and reacts to the feelings of failure or heartbreak. The problem is the person responding reacts by doing what they think is the correct thing.

As we looked at each of the promises given to Adam, Abraham, Jacob, Joseph, Moses, Samson and Peter, we will note that each promise was different, yet the process they went through to receive their promises is similar and it is this process or pattern we are studying. If we can learn from their experiences, this pattern of how they went from promise given to promise received will help us to receive more of our promises.

Adam

Let's look at Adam. We all know the first promise given to Adam had to do with not eating from the fruit of the Tree of Knowledge of Good and Evil. Once Adam ate the fruit, the promise was fulfilled by God and death became a reality. Adam immediately knew good and evil evidenced to us in

Scripture as found in Genesis 3:7-8:

7 Then the eyes of both of them were opened and they knew that they were naked; so they sewed fig leaves together and made for themselves loin-coverings. 8 And they heard the sound of ADONAI Elohim going to and fro in the garden in the wind of the day. So the man and his wife hid themselves from the presence of ADONAI Elohim in the in the midst of the Tree of the garden.

Once Adam realized God did exactly what He said he would do, there was a change in Adam. This change is what in this book we will refer to as the Breaking. The Breaking is an experience in which one who has received a promise from God and then fails or sins, is then broken by the experience and is contrite. In the case of Adam and Eve, their first reaction to their sin against God was the exact opposite of what God wanted. By the way, this is a universal truth that when we react to our Breaking, we will almost always do the wrong thing.

Adam and Eve clearly feel broken and they react by

deciding to sew leaves into garments and then hid themselves from God. Or at least attempt to hide themselves from Him. Notice the Breaking has a significant effect on Adam and Eve and their reaction was to do something to fix their situation. The Breaking will cause us to look to ourselves for the answer to our problem, how to restore ourselves to a position to where we can once again be eligible to receive the promise God has given to us.

The first choice we see Adam make after receiving the knowledge of Good and Evil was to choose evil. One might ask, how is it evil to sew garments out of leaves and hide because you know you are naked? The answer is that anytime we try to cover our sin by our own efforts it is evil. We know Adam understood this to some extent because if covering himself were adequate, why would he then feel the need to hide?

The Breaking will always bring changes we think will be helpful. But is a wasted effort, causing us to repent of more in the end. In Adam's case we only read about one Breaking event after his fall.

Abraham

Abraham is different as we see several Breaking events after his promises were given. It is interesting Abraham is called the father of the faithful when we see such a struggle at times in his walking in faith.

As we review Abraham's promises, we know God told him he was to become a great nation but at the time he was 75 years old and childless. So what does Abraham do? He brings Lot, his nephew along with him even though God told him to leave all his relatives behind. This failure of faith brings Abraham's first Breaking into play. In Genesis chapter 13:5-7:

5 Now Lot, who was going with Abram, also had sheep and cattle and tents, 6 so that the land could not support them living together, because their possessions were many, and they were not able to stay together. 7 So there was a quarrel between the shepherds of Abram's livestock and the shepherds of Lot's livestock. (Now the Canaanites and the Perizzites were living in the land then).

When we read these verses, we often overlook just how emotionally painful this experience must have been for Abraham. After all, it appears as if Abraham considers Lot a possible heir and treated him as a son. Now because of Abraham's disobedience to God, he is going through the Breaking of separation from Lot.

However, the Breaking caused by Abraham's choice to bring Lot with him and the separation from Lot still doesn't bring Abraham to a place of complete faith, as it concerns his promise of becoming a great nation. In Genesis 15:1-6 we read a dialogue between Abraham and God:

1 After these things the word of ADONAI came to Abram in a vision saying, "Do not fear, Abram. I am your shield, your very great reward. 2 But Abram said, "My Lord ADONAI, what will You give me, since I am living without children, and the heir of my household is Eliezer of Damascus? 3 Then Abram said, "Look! You have given me no seed, so a house-born servant is my heir. 4 Then behold, the word of ADONAI came to him saying, "This one will not be your heir, but in fact, one who will come from your own body will be your heir. 5

He took him outside and said, "Look up now, at the sky, and count the stars—if you are able to count them." Then He said to him, "So shall your seed be. 6 Then he believed in ADONAI and He reckoned it to him as righteousness.

Even though separated from Lot, Abraham is looking for ways to help God to keep His promise and offers to make Eliezer an heir, because he and Sarah are still without children. But God answers Abraham by telling him to look at the stars because his seed would be as the stars.
It is important to notice that verse 6 says that Abraham believed and his belief was reckoned or counted as righteousness.

Yet after the Breaking caused by separation from Lot and the second Breaking after God turns down the Eliezer option, Abraham though believing that God would fulfill His promises still thought he needed to assist him to accomplish his promise.

In Genesis 16:1-3 we find his next attempt at helping God.

1 Now Sarai, Abram's wife, had not borne him children. But she had an Egyptian slave-girl—her name was Hagar. 2 So Sarai said to Abram, "Look now, ADONAI has prevented me from having children. Go, please, to my slave-girl. Perhaps I'll get a son by her." Abram listened to Sarai's voice. 3 So Sarai, Abram's wife, took her slave-girl Hagar the Egyptian—after Abram had lived ten years in the land of Canaan—and gave her to Abram her husband to be his wife.

This plan is conceived by Sarai his wife, but Abraham is a willing participant in the plan and the result is the birth of Ishmael. Any Bible student knows, this brought significant difficulties later in the Bible effecting Abraham's descendants. But for the purpose of this section, we will look at the Breaking that takes place in Genesis 17:15-16:

15 God also said to Abraham, "As for Sarai your wife, you shall not call her by the name Sarai. Rather, Sarah is her name. 16 And I will bless her, and moreover, I will give you a son from her. I will bless her and she will give rise to nations. Kings of the peoples will come from her.

This particular breaking is unique because it begins with a new promise being given to Abraham and Sarah. The addition of the promise that Kings of Nations would come from Sarah.

Abraham, who is known for his faith and who was called righteous because he had believed what God promised him, responds in doubt and unbelief complete with falling down laughter in Genesis 17:17-18:

17 Then Abraham fell on his face and laughed, and said to his heart, "Will a son be born to a 100-year-old man? Or will Sarah—who is 90 years old—give birth? 18 So Abraham said to God, "If only Ishmael might live before you!

Remember Abraham first receive his promise when he was 75 years old and now he is 99 years old. 24 years had passed and no child of the promise was born.

He pleads with God one more time. Won't Ishmael suffice to fulfill the promise?

But God responds strongly: Genesis 17:19:

17:19 But God said, "On the contrary, Sarah your wife will bear you a son and you must name him Isaac. So I will confirm My covenant with him as an everlasting covenant for his seed after him.

Said another way, Isaac will be born to prove I will always keep my covenants and promises. Then Abraham endures another Breaking found in Genesis 21, when Sarah tells him to send his son Ishmael and his mother Hagar away.

21:10 So she said to Abraham, "Drive out this female slave and her son, for the son of this female slave will not be an heir with my son—with Isaac.11 Now the matter was very displeasing in Abraham's eyes on account of his son.12 But God said to Abraham, "Do not be displeased about the boy and your slave woman. Whatever Sarah says to you, listen to her voice. For through Isaac shall your seed be called.

You can feel the heartbreaking in Abraham's displeasure in verse 1 But God tells Abraham not to be displeased because Isaac was the promise Abraham was given not Ishmael.

Each of these Breaking events in Abraham's life were caused simply because Abraham believed God's promises were true, but believed he was in some way responsible to assist God in bringing the promises to pass. Finally after four separate Breakings, Abraham was ready to believe fully in God's ability to do everything He promised all without Abraham's help.

We read more about this struggle in the often misinterpreted series of verse found in Galatians 4:21-31:

21 Tell me, you who want to be under Torah, don't you understand the Torah? 22 For it is written that Abraham had two sons, one by the slave woman and one by the free woman. 23 But one—the son by the slave woman—was born naturally; while the other—the son by the free woman—was through the promise. 24 Now these things are being treated allegorically, for these are two covenants. One is from Mount Sinai, giving birth to slavery—this is Hagar. 25 But this Hagar is Mount Sinai in Arabia and corresponds to the present Jerusalem, for she is in slavery along with her children. 26 But the Jerusalem above is free—she is our mother. 27 For it is written: "Rejoice, O barren woman who bears no children. Break forth and shout, you who suffer no labor pains. For more are the children of the desolate than of the one who has a husband. 28 Now you, brethren—like Isaac, you are children of promise. 29 But just as at that time the one born according to the flesh persecuted the one born according to the Ruach, so it is now. 30 But what does the Scripture say? "Drive out the slave woman and her son, for the son of the slave woman shall not inherit with the son" of the free woman. 31 So then, brethren, we are not children of the slave woman but of the free woman.

Too often these verses are used to prop up an argument that there is a battle between Torah and Grace. When the truth is these texts are simply about knowing God can and will fulfill His promises to set us free from the bondage of sin. The writer said we should learn a lesson from Abraham and allow God to do what He has promised without our help. In other words, if we were able to follow the Torah perfectly, our efforts in the flesh would not nor could not save us or anyone else. We are only redeemed completely by the provision of Yeshua's atonement. Who, as God became flesh and dwelt among us, living, dying and resurrecting to provide the promise.

Just as Abraham thought he had to physically assist God in bringing forth an heir first Lot, Eliezer and finally Ishmael. His efforts through the flesh brought forth only a child of bondage. God warned us our efforts to assist Him are unfruitful, brings bondage to our lives and demonstrates a lack of trust in His ability to do all He promised to do.

Jacob

Moving from Abraham to Jacob, we find what may be the most dramatic and easily recognizable example of "The Breaking" in the Bible. As we begin looking into Jacob's experience, we remember God had given Jacob four promises as he was running from Esau's wrath. Jacob spends 21 years at Laban's home and leaves with his wives Rachael and Leah and his children and all of the wealth he has obtained. It is very important for us to note that while Jacob was with Laban, he demonstrated great faith in God's ability to provide and protect him while there. As evidenced by the conversation between Jacob and Laban in Genesis 30:27-30:

27 But Laban said to him, "If I've found favor in your eyes—I've looked for good omens, and ADONAI has blessed me because of you. 28 Moreover he said, "Name your own price and I'll pay it. 29 Then he said to him, "You yourself know how I've served you and how your livestock fared with me. 30 For you had very little before I came, and it has been busting at the seams in abundance. So ADONAI blessed you with my every step. So now, when am I myself going to make something for my household also?

In these verses it is Laban that makes the first comment about Jacob's blessings coming from God. Then Jacob states God had blessed his every step. To simplify, the testimony of both Jacob and Laban speak of God keeping three of the four promises He made to Jacob.

God also protected Jacob when Laban tried to cheat him out of his payment in livestock by making the sheep and goats prosperous. Genesis 30:39-43:

39 the flocks mated near the branches, and the flocks gave birth to striped, spotted and colorful ones. 40 Now Jacob separated the lambs and set the faces of the flocks toward the striped ones as well as all the dark-colored ones among Laban's flocks.

Then he set aside the herds for himself and did not put them with Laban's flocks. 41 Whenever the strong flocks mated, Jacob put the branches in the watering troughs before the eyes of the flocks, to have them mate near the branches. 42 But when the flocks were sickly, he did not put the branches down—so the sickly ones became Laban's and the stronger ones became Jacob's. 43 And the man grew exceedingly prosperous and had numerous flocks, along with female and male servants, camels and donkeys.

Jacob, like Abraham, believed God's promises and had no

difficulty believing He is able to keep his promises. That is three of the four promises given to Jacob by God when Jacob dreamed of the ladder to Heaven.

Jacob's Breaking comes on his way home to the promised land as he prepares to see his brother again; which we find beginning in Genesis 32:4-7:

4 Then Jacob sent messengers before him to his brother Esau, to the land of Seir, the field of Edom. 5 He also commanded them saying, "This is what you should say to my lord, to Esau: 'This is what your servant Jacob said: I've been staying with Laban, and have lingered until now. 6 Now I've come to possess oxen and donkeys, flocks, male servants and female servants. I sent word to tell my lord, in order to find favor in your eyes.' 7 The messengers returned to Jacob saying, "We went to your brother, to Esau, and he's also coming out to meet you—and 400 men with him.

Jacob sent his messengers to see if God had prepared the way for him to go home. After all, God promised he would be brought safely home again. Instead, he receives the report that Esau was on the way with 400 men. Clearly from Jacob's perspective God had failed. As a result of this Jacob is going to take matters into his own hands and help out. So Jacob devised a plan in which he divided his herds to send them ahead with instructions of what to say when they reach Esau.

Genesis 32:18-19:

18 Then he commanded the first one saying, "When my brother Esau meets you and asks you saying, 'To whom do you belong, and where are you going, and to whom do all these before you belong?' 19 then you are to say, 'To your servant, to Jacob—it's an offering sent to my lord, to Esau. And look, he's also behind us.'

Imagine how heartbreaking the experience of having to choose which of your wives and children to send in which group if Esau attacked where some may survive.

It was not until after Jacob established his own plan that he turns to God in prayers in Genesis 32:10-13:

10 Then Jacob said, "O God of my father Abraham, and God of my father Isaac, ADONAI, who said to me,

'Return to your land and to your relatives and I will do good with you.' 11 I am unworthy of all the proofs of mercy and of all the dependability that you have shown to your servant. For with only my staff I crossed over this Jordan, and now I've become two camps. 12 Deliver me, please, from my brother's hand, from Esau's hand, for I'm afraid of him that he'll come and strike me—the mothers with the children. 13 You Yourself said, 'I will most certainly do good with you, and will make your seed like the sand of the sea that cannot be counted because of its abundance.'

Feeling as if he had to make the choice of which wives and which children to place in danger had to be heart wrenching, and a Breaking in Jacob's life which brought him to prayer, reminding God of his promises. In his prayer we find Jacob reminding God of His promises and covenants. Genesis 32:25-32:

25 So Jacob remained all by himself. Then a man wrestled with him until the break of dawn.26 When He saw that He had not overcome him, He struck the socket of his hip, so He dislocated the socket of

Jacob's hip when He wrestled with him.27 Then He said, "Let Me go, for the dawn has broken." But he said, "I won't let You go unless You bless me."28 Then He said to him, "What is your name?" "Jacob," he said.29 Then He said, "Your name will no longer be Jacob, but rather Israel, for you have struggled with God and with men, and you have overcome."30 Then Jacob asked and said, "Please tell me Your name." But He said, "What's this—you are asking My name?" Then He blessed him there.31 So Jacob named the place Peniel, "for I've seen God face to face, and my life has been spared."32 Now the sun rose upon him just as he crossed by Peniel—limping because of his hip.

The wrestling match with God is one of the clearest examples of Breaking in the life of a Biblical character. We see Jacob actually wrestling in what commentators say is a battle between the old man Jacob and the new man Israel. The breaking comes as the man touches Jacob's hip and just as the legs of the thief were broken, Jacobs hip was set out of joint, causing Jacob's life to be changed completely. He was never able to walk the same way again. This battle, which lasted until morning, was the last phase in the

Breaking of Jacob. From his deceptive beginning, through his experience being deceived, first by marrying Leah instead of Rachael, continuing through Laban's attempt to cheat Jacob out of his wages, until the moment when he is completely broken, it is hard to find a more physical/spiritual example of Breaking in the Bible.

Joseph

In Joseph's dream he was promised he would rise to a place of authority over his whole family. He found himself sharing his dream with his brothers rather than his promise being immediately fulfilled.

His brothers scheme to kill him. Only after somewhat cooler heads prevail, he is instead sold into slavery. Talk about a moment of Breaking. As we continue to look at Joseph's life in Egypt, nowhere do we find Joseph's situation causing him to reject God and His promises. However, this does not mean Joseph doesn't continue to go through the Breaking process. His Breaking continues from being sold into slavery, to being falsely accused of attempted rape.

Then after being promised by the cupbearer he would help him out, he still remains in prison for two more years. Each of these events were used by God to bring Joseph to the place of Breaking where he could humbly stand, not only before his brothers, but before Pharaoh and all Egypt. As he would ultimately become the viceroy, second only to the Pharaoh. Just imagine Joseph's response to being raised up to that position if he still thought of himself the way he did when he first told his brothers about his dream. Joseph never stopped believing in God and in the promise of his dream, even while within the depths of prison. But in order for him to become the man he would become, Joseph needed to go through his Breaking.

Moses

Like Joseph, Moses endures his Breaking while on his journey, in the same locations to and from Egypt. Moses also endured several Breakings with the first one happening when God is preparing Moses to go to Egypt and speak to both the people of Israel and Pharaoh. Moses begins arguing with God about his ability to speak on God's behalf. We read in Exodus 4:13-16 of the interchange between the two:

14 Then the anger of Adonai was kindled against Moses, so He said, "In fact, Aaron the Levite is your brother. I know that he can speak well. Moreover, he is on his way to meet you! When he sees you, he will be glad in his heart.15 You are to speak to him and put the words in his mouth. I will be with your mouth and with his, and teach you what to do. 16 He will be your spokesman to the people, so that he may act as a mouthpiece for you, and it will be as if you were as God for him.

During his Breaking, Moses angers God and, as a result, God removes from Moses the position of spokesman and gives it to Aaron. This action removes Moses from the opportunity to be used by God in a unique way. As God desired to show His power through Moses' weakness. Instead, Moses is replaced by Aaron who speaks well. Aaron replacing Moses in this way took away the demonstration of God empowering Moses beyond his natural ability. The Breaking continues only a few verses later when Moses is confronted by God because he has not circumcised his sons in Exodus 4:24-26:

*24 **It happened along the way, at a lodging place, that Adonai met him and sought to kill him.** 25 But Zipporah took a flint, cut off the foreskin of her son, and threw it at his feet, saying, "You are surely a bridegroom of blood to me." 26 She said, "A bridegroom of blood" because of the circumcision. Then He let him alone.*

We are not told in Scripture why Moses had not brought his sons into the covenant of circumcision. But we can deduce from the text his wife Zipporah was part of the reason. As she has such a violent reaction to God's strong response to Moses' failure. This Breaking was severe because Moses' non-compliance almost cost him his life.

The next series of Breakings are often thought of in terms of affects on the Egyptians. These are known as the Ten Plagues and were used by God to not only Break the Egyptian Pharaoh and the people of Egypt, but also to break Moses. Remember when God called Moses He said the following in Exodus 3:12:

12 So He said, "I will surely be with you. So that will be the sign to you that it is I who have sent you. When you have brought the people out of Egypt: you will worship God on this mountain."

Notice God tells Moses He will be with him as a sign to him. The plagues were given one after another to show God's power to Moses and to show Moses God is always with Him. The need for this Breaking of Moses is evident in Moses' response. Instead of Pharaoh letting the Children of Israel go at his request things indeed got harder. They would not only have to make bricks but they would also have to gather the materials to make them, while having to achieve the same quotas each day. The response of the leaders of Israel was to condemn Moses for making things worse and Moses' response to God shows a need for increased faith. Exodus 5:22-23:

22 So Moses returned to Adonai and said, "Adonai, why have You brought evil on these people? Is this why You sent me? 23 Ever since I came to Pharaoh to speak in Your Name, he has brought evil on these people. You have not delivered Your people at all."

Moses continues to go through his Breaking as he learns God's ways are higher than our ways. The more we see Moses endure, the more we see God Breaking Moses from his lack of self-esteem. Teaching Moses, God's promises are always true no matter what the outcome seems like while God is accomplishing his purposes.

In Romans 8:28 we see this written another way:

28 Now we know that all things work together for good for those who love God, who are called according to His purpose.

"Called according to His purpose" is another way of saying God has called them and given a promise that He will fulfill for their good or blessing.

Ephesians 3:20 says it this way:

20 Now to Him who is able to do far beyond all that we ask or imagine, by means of His power that works in us,

Moses is unique. His story is about learning to let God bring about His promises. In Moses' case, he doubted his personal ability and asked God to let someone else lead the Children of Israel out of bondage. The lesson is the same. Man cannot fulfill a promise for God. But the direction of the lesson comes from opposite sides.

When Moses complained to God. Not only had He not delivered the Children of Israel, but the situation had worsened. God answered Moses again with the following words from Exodus 6:1-5:

1 Adonai said to Moses, "Now you will see what I am going to do to Pharaoh. By way of a strong hand he will let them go, and drive them out of his land."2 God spoke further to Moses and said to him, "I am Adonai.3 I appeared to Abraham, to Isaac and to Jacob, as El Shaddai. Yet by My Name, Adonai, I made Myself known to them.4 I also established My covenant with them, to give them the land of Canaan, the land of their pilgrimage where they journeyed.

5 Furthermore, I have heard the groaning of Bnei-Yisrael, whom the Egyptians are keeping in bondage. So I have remembered My covenant.

In this text, God reminds Moses one more time that he would see what God was going to do to Egypt. God also reminds Moses that He is a covenant or promise keeping God. But furthering the Breaking of Moses is something easily overlooked as one reads through Exodus Chapter 6. Take a look at the first 10 verses and count how many times God uses the word "I." Over and over God is reminding Moses the situation is about God and God alone. But as we continue to read, we see Moses still thinking about himself. In Exodus 6: 9-12:

9 Moses spoke this way to Bnei-Yisrael, but they did not listen to him because of their broken spirit and cruel bondage.10 So Adonai told Moses, 11 "Go, speak to Pharaoh king of Egypt, so that will he let Bnei-Yisrael go out of his land." 12 But Moses said to Adonai, "Bnei-Yisrael have not listened to me. So how would Pharaoh listen to me—I, who have uncircumcised lips?

Moses obeys God and relays the message to the Children of Israel but because of their broken spirit and cruel bondage they would not listen. Moses' response to God's instructions in verse 12 lets us know that Moses didn't trust God completely. He was concerned with Pharaoh listening to him. While he should have been concerned with Pharaoh listening to God.

In verse 30, Moses repeats the phrase "I am of uncircumcised lips." Exodus 6:30:

30 But Moses said to Adonai, "I am of uncircumcised lips, so how would Pharaoh listen to me?"

By saying this, Moses is reminding God he didn't fully believe in His covenant promise. Notice it was his lips that were uncircumcised. He was saying Pharaoh won't believe what I say because I don't believe it myself.

After the 10 plagues are completed, we see a change in Moses. Not as much as a result of anything Moses does, but because of what he says and the response of the Children of Israel. Exodus 12:28:

143

28 Then Bnei-Yisrael went and did it. They did just as Adonai had commanded Moses and Aaron.

Notice this is the first time Moses tells the Children of Israel to do something and they immediately respond as God commanded. A change or Breaking happened in Moses; he now spoke with authority. He now believed what God promised and because of that the Children of Israel believed and obeyed.

Samson

We remember Samson's promise was given through his parents before he was born Samson also had requirements in order for his promise to be fulfilled. As we read through the book of Judges, we get introduced to Samson, and the first thing we learn about him is found in Judges 13:24:

24 Then the woman bore a son, and called his name Samson. So the boy grew up and Adonai blessed him.

Notice the text says that the boy grew up. Samson has become an adult, and until Judges 13:24, he is blessed by God. Samson's adult life is not filled with holiness and righteousness. He gets involved with women who are not part of Israel. He is continually deceived by foreign women. He reacts to the trickeries violently and ultimately is captured, blinded and imprisoned.

Then we come to Judges 16:23-26 when we see Samson's Breaking.

23 Now the Philistine lords gathered to offer a great sacrifice to Dagon their god and to celebrate, as they said, "Our god has given our enemy Samson into our hand." 24 When the people saw him, they praised their god, as they said, "Our god has given into our hand our enemy and the destroyer of our country, who has slain many of us." 25 Now it came about when their hearts were merry that they said, "Call for Samson, that he may amuse us." So they called for Samson from the prison, and he did make them laugh, when they made him stand between the pillars.

26 Then Samson said to the lad that held him by the hand, "Let me feel the pillars on which the temple rests, so I may lean on them."

It should be noted that Samson's Breaking didn't come as a result of the many deceptions and battles he fought. The breaking comes when the Philistines proclaim to offer sacrifice to their false god celebrating Dagon's ability to hand Samson, their enemy, over to them and mocking Samson.

This action which demeaned both Samson and the God of Israel brought Samson to the point of breaking. Samson reacts as a broken man in Judges 16:27-28:

27 Now the temple was full of men and women. All the Philistine lords were there and about 3,000 men and women on the roof looking on while Samson was amusing them. 28 Then Samson called out to Adonai and said, "My Lord Adonai, please remember me and please strengthen me only this once, O God, so that I may this once take revenge on the Philistines for my two eyes."

The mighty Samson finds himself being used to entertain the Philistines while they worship their idol. It is more than he can take and in his brokenness, he turns to God and prays asking for strength one more time, to take revenge on his enemies.

John 21:15-17:

15 When they had finished breakfast, Yeshua said to Simon Peter, "Simon, son of John, do you love Me more than these?" "Yes, Lord," he said to Him, "You know that I love you." He said to him, "Feed My lambs!" 16 He said to him again a second time, "Simon, son of John, do you love Me?" "Yes, Lord," he said, "You know that I love You." He said to him, "Take care of My sheep!" 17 He said to him a third time, "Simon, son of John, do you love Me?" Peter was grieved because He said to him for a third time, "Do you love Me?" And he said to Him, "Lord, You know everything! You know that I love You!" Yeshua said to him, "Feed My sheep!"

We read about the breaking of Peter as Yeshua asks Peter if he loves Him. Peter, like many of us who believe we love God, base our belief on our feelings. We will say we know in our hearts we love God. The problem with this thought process is the Bible tells us we cannot fully know our hearts. Jeremiah 17:9

9 "The heart is deceitful above all things, and incurable—who can know it?

The truth is only God knows what's in our hearts. Which is revealed to Peter when he finds out in the conversation he has with Yeshua.

In in verse 17, Peter is grieved or broken hearted because Yeshua asked him about his love for a third time.
His response to this Breaking was an affirmation of his submission to Yeshua as Lord. It is also interesting this event happens after the second experience Peter has with Yeshua, telling him to go fishing after catching no fish

through his own efforts. The connection between the two fishing experiences and the "do you love me?" questions clearly shows us Peter was still depending upon his own abilities and strength. In the book of John, we find Peter being grieved or "broken' by the realization he had not fully submitted to the authority of God in every aspect of his life.

Eric

Once I had my promise from God, I began to do the same thing most people do when they hear from Him. I started to make plans to help fulfill His promise. I began to write letters to my parents showing them all the prophecies about the Messiah. I began to plan every phone call to my mother so that somehow I could manipulate Yeshua into the discussion. I believed my mother was not in relationship with God in the way I believed she should be. I also knew I had a promise from God, that she would come to faith in Yeshua. Thus, I put every effort into helping God to keep His word.

My interaction with my mother and my family became

stressful and strained. Dinners became Bible studies, and family events became debating sessions. To my surprise, my best efforts were rejected and instead of my mother and family opening their minds and hearts in response to my presentation of Yeshua, there was only a greater gulf between us.

I didn't understand why this was happening. I knew God had spoken to my heart and I know God doesn't lie. I also knew the Bible instructs us to be witnesses and to share Messiah with those who don't yet know Him. I was doing exactly what I believed I was supposed to but the results were not what I wanted or expected to, happen. Instead of bringing my mother to belief in Yeshua, all of my efforts were causing her to reject Him.

It was breaking my heart our relationship went from great to difficult. Not only didn't she enjoy being with me, but the truth was I became so frustrated with trying so hard I began avoiding conversations just so I would avoid my own failures. I didn't understand why, if I was doing everything I was directed to do, the results were not coming to pass.

It was at this point I stopped to examine the idea. Maybe, I was only doing what came easiest to do. I realized very quickly that while I was sharing what I believed, my actions and plans were completely based upon what *I* could do to bring my mother to faith. I was trying to get my mother to believe in Yeshua, but everything I did was based not on His redeeming power but instead, it was about me and what I was doing to save my mother.

This realization was heartbreaking. I knew it was true that my efforts to share my relationship with God, through the atonement of Yeshua with my mother was happening without actually introducing her to God through Yeshua. I was telling her all about what the Bible says and sharing prophesy and fulfillment, but I forgot what 2nd Corinthians 3:3-6 says:

3 It is clear that you are a letter from Messiah delivered by us—written not with ink but with the Ruach of the living God, not on tablets of stone but on tablets of human hearts. 4 Such is the confidence we have through Messiah toward God—5 not that we are competent in ourselves to consider anything as coming from ourselves, but our competence is from God. 6 He also made us competent as servants of a new covenant—not of the letter, but of the Ruach. For the letter kills, but the Ruach gives life.

The Breaking Questions

1) Can you think of examples of Breakings in your life?

2) Can you think of a Breaking you responded well to?

3) Can you think of a Breaking you didn't respond well to?

4) Can you think of any Breakings that you have experienced more then once?

5) Was there a Breaking that you recognized while experiencing it?

The Death

The Death is found after the criminal's legs were broken, he died. This death was not just physical. It was spiritual as well. In Luke 23, this criminal had completely submitted his life into the hands of God, including His will for his life. Not only did he desire God's will but he also desired to be in the presence of God. He had completely become a new man dying to self-will, self-desire, self-assurance and self-reliance.

This death is expressed in the Book of Romans 12:1-2:

1 I urge you therefore, brothers and sisters, by the mercies of God, to present your bodies as a living sacrifice—holy, acceptable to God—which is your spiritual service. 2 Do not be conformed to this world but be transformed by the renewing of your mind, so that you may discern what is the will of God—what is good and acceptable and perfect.

In this passage we are instructed to present ourselves as a

living sacrifice. This means we have to do just as this criminal did and die to our own will and submit fully to God's will for our life. It is only when we completely die to self, that we can have a renewed mind to discern what is God's will for our lives.

The Death is a moment in time after a "breaking" when the subject or character fully submits to the will of God in their lives. This dying to one's self is always the precursor to God releasing the fullness of His blessings into the life of the one who comes to that place spiritually where they die.

In John 3:30 we read where John the Immerser said:

30 He must increase, while I must decrease."

Paul said in 1 Corinthians 15:31:

I die every day—yes, as surely as the boast in you, brothers and sisters, which I have in Messiah Yeshua our Lord.

We read about this in terms of being born again in Roman 6:5-11:

5 For if we have become joined together in the likeness of His death, certainly we also will be joined together in His resurrection—6 knowing our old man was crucified with Him so that the sinful body might be done away with, so we no longer serve sin. 7 For he who has died is set free from sin. 8 Now if we have died with Messiah, we believe that we shall also live with Him. 9 We know that Messiah, having been raised from the dead, no longer dies; death no longer is master over Him.10 For the death He died, He died to sin once for all; but the life He lives, He lives to God. 11 So also continually count yourselves both dead to sin and alive to God in Messiah Yeshua.

Adam

The death in the pattern in Adam's life comes when he is cast out of the garden and no longer has access to the Tree of Life, which provided fruit in which he and all those who would eat of it would live forever. His Breaking came when he realized his sin and his reaction was to sew clothing from leaves and hide from God. His next reaction is to blame God for his failure which we read in Genesis 3:12:

12 Then the man said, "The woman whom You gave to be with me—she gave me of the Tree, and I ate."

Although Adam had been broken and realized his sin, he still had not completely surrendered himself to God. It isn't until Adam hears his punishment, that he is finally brought to the place of spiritual self-death. We see evidence of this taking place when Adam removes the coverings he fashioned out of leaves and puts on the tunics skins God made. Therefore demonstrating his understanding he could not adequately cover his sinful actions. Adam's relinquishment of his life demonstrated his surrendered will and life to God. Genesis 3:21:

21 Adonai Elohim made Adam and his wife tunics of skin and He clothed them.

Adam was the first man and the first example of man believing he had the ability to do something to effect changes to what God had promised by his own efforts and abilities. This false notion of assisting God or even the possibility for us to assist God in keeping His promises, becomes a consistent issue throughout Scripture. As we see with Adam and will continue to see as we study Abraham and the balance of our seven subjects.

After Adam submitted his will to God and died spiritually, he was also expelled from the Garden of Eden and with this separation from the Tree of Life he would also now die physically. Genesis 3:24:

24 *And He expelled the man; and at the east of the Garden of Eden He had cheruvim dwell along, with the whirling sword of flame, to guard the way to the Tree of Life.*

This death and separation changed everything in Adam's life, his relationship to his wife and his family. "You shall surely die," wasn't just a figurative statement, but it became a reality. The day they ate of the fruit in rebellion brought about physical death. The day he ate the fruit, He also gave Adam the opportunity to die spiritually and in doing so, allowed God to restore the relationship between himself and God.

Abraham

As we continue our study, we come to Abraham. We remember his acceptance of God at his calling to leave his homeland and family and travel to a new country. His promise of having many children and his breaking at each attempt to help God to bring His promises to pass, first with Lot, then with Elezer and ending with Ishmael led to the moment of Abraham's spiritual death. In this case, the Bible actually provides a verse in which we see this personal, spiritual death take place. Genesis 17:3-5:

3 Abram fell on his face, and God spoke with him, saying,
4 "For My part, because My covenant is with you, you will be the father of a multitude of nations. 5 No longer will your name be Abram, but your name will be Abraham, because I make you the father of a multitude of nations.

In verse 3, we see Abraham fall on his face in submission and honor, followed by God's reiteration of His covenant promises. Then in verse 5, we see the evidence of the death of Abram as God changes his name from Abram to Abraham. How do we know this change of name brought the spiritual death of Abraham? Let us look at Genesis 18:9-10, when God has the following conversation with Abraham during dinner.

9 Then they said to him, "Where is Sarah your wife?" "There, in the tent," he said.10 Then He said, "I will most surely return to you in about a year's time, surprisingly, Sarah your wife will have a son." Sarah was listening at the entrance of the tent, which was behind Him.

Notice there is no mention of Abraham showing any doubt or coming up with a new plan to assist God with the process of Sarah conceiving and having a son. Previously, Abraham questions how God was going to fulfill his promise. But this time no doubt, no questions and no plans. Abram had died and now Abraham lives.

Jacob

Jacob provides us with a unique example that is very important for us to understand as we apply the Pattern to our lives. Sometimes we have to go through the cycle more than once in our life. In Jacob, we find at least two clear examples of where He goes through the cycle. In application, we may have to relearn our lessons over and over until we come to victory over ourselves once and for all. Jacob's first death is found after he deceived his father and brother and is running for his life. Remember, Jacob's promise was the promise of inheritance and lineage. He was to be the recipient of the birthright and all that included. Even though he had accepted that God was God and his promise had been given, Jacob schemes twice to acquire his promise through his own effort. First with the red beans he trades with Esau for the birthright. It is important to remember that according to God, the birthright did not belong to Esau to begin with. The second time is when he presents himself to Isaac pretending to be Esau and "steals" the blessing. I said "he steals" because it is not possible to steal something that already belongs to you.

It is after this second deception we find Jacob experiencing his first death. We find this in Genesis chapter 28:11-22:

11 He happened upon a certain place and spent the night there, for the sun had set. So he took one of the stones from the place and put it by his head and lay down in that place. 12 He dreamed: All of a sudden, there was a stairway set up on the earth and its top reaching to the heavens—and behold, angels of God going up and down on it! 13 Surprisingly, Adonai was standing on top of it and He said, "I am Adonai, the God of your father Abraham and the God of Isaac. The land on which you lie, I will give it to you and to your seed. 14 Your seed will be as the dust of the land, and you will burst forth to the west and to the east and to the north and to the south. And in you all the families of the earth will be blessed—and in your seed 15 Behold, I am with you, and I will watch over you wherever you go, and I will bring you back to this land, for I will not forsake you until I have done what I promised you." 16 Jacob woke up from his sleep and said, "Undoubtedly, Adonai is in this place—and I was unaware." 17 So he was afraid and said, "How fearsome this place is! This is none other than the House of God—this must be the gate of heaven!"

18 Early in the morning Jacob got up and took the stone, which he had placed by his head, and set it up as a memorial stone and poured oil on top of it.

19 He called the name of that place Beth-El (though originally the city's name was Luz). 20 Then Jacob made a vow saying, "If God will be with me and watch over me on this way that I am going, and provide me food to eat and clothes to wear, 21 and I return in shalom to my father's house, then Adonai will be my God. 22 So this stone which I set up as a memorial stone will become God's House, and of everything You provide me I will definitely give a tenth of it to You."

Notice Jacob lies down and has a dream. This symbolic dying experience is when Jacob responds to the dream by rising up a new man. As a new man he sets up a memorial altar and makes a vow to honor God in all he does and with all he possess or comes to possess. He ends the experience by sharing his heart's desire to return to his home.

Joseph

As we follow the life of Joseph. We see him from a young boy who was spoiled by his father through his early years of dreaming and interacting with his brothers. Through his time in slavery, being falsely accused by Potiphar's wife and imprisoned; being released from prison and raised up to be the second in command of Egypt, we find Joseph being blessed by God. His life is one of the best examples of this five-part pattern recurring. One of the clearest examples of Joseph's "death" is found in Genesis 43:30:

Then Joseph hurried out because his compassion grew warm and tender toward his brother so that he wanted to cry. So he went into an inner room and wept there.

Joseph is at the end of his journey from his father's house to the fulfillment of the promise God had given him as a child. He has been blessed in many ways and has risen to the top of Egyptian society. He had everything the world had to offer. He had reconnected with his brothers and exercised his authority over them and his father Jacob. Yet it isn't until this moment when he sees his brother and is overcome with compassion that he fully dies to himself. Before this moment, he was the viceroy of Egypt demonstrating his authority over his brothers. It isn't until he finally dies to himself that he is revealed as Joseph and in this humility he becomes the prophesied ruler that uses his power not to punish but to preserve.

Moses

Moses is one of the most exciting characters in the Bible. Beginning at his birth, being saved when all males babies where being thrown into the Nile to their death, we read of his salvation in the very same river by the Pharaoh's daughter. He is reared in the palace as the son of Pharaoh and then chooses to be counted and suffer with the Children of Israel instead of being heir to the King of Egypt. He ends up herding sheep in Midian and while there experiences an introduction to the God of Israel as a voice projected from a fiery bush. Each of these events alone would make an excellent movie script; placed all together the details demonstrate God's involvement in Moses' life from before he was born. A close reading will expose the Pattern being exhibited throughout his life. As with others we have discussed earlier, Moses had many examples of when he died to self. I want to point out only one of them in this book. In Exodus chapter 12-14, we find the calling and the interaction between Moses and God and Israel and between Moses and Pharaoh. As you read these passages, you will find God speaking to Moses and Moses then repeating what God said to either Israel or Pharaoh. In between, you often find Moses showing faith in God but doubt in himself to the point when God actually allows Moses to replace himself in part with Aaron because Moses didn't feel qualified to be the spokesman of God. Then we come to Exodus 14:13-18:

13 But Moses said to the people, "Don't be afraid! Stand still, and see the salvation of Adonai, which He will perform for you today. You have seen the Egyptians today, but you will never see them again, ever! 14 Adonai will fight for you, while you hold your peace." 15 Then Adonai said to Moses, "Why are you crying to Me? Tell Bnei-Yisrael to go forward. 16 Lift up your staff, stretch out your hand over the sea, and divide it. Then Bnei-Yisrael will go into the midst of the sea on dry ground. 17 Then I, behold, I will harden the hearts of the Egyptians, and they will go in after them, so that I will be glorified over Pharaoh and all his army, his chariots and his horsemen. 18 Then the Egyptians will know that I am Adonai, when I have been glorified over Pharaoh, his chariots and his horsemen."

As we read these words of text, we notice a first in the interaction between Moses and Israel and God. This is the first time Moses answers the people in faith, trusting only in God to respond. Moses spoke in full authority, "don't be afraid," "Stand still and see," "God will fight for you." Notice the words in verse 15 where God tells Moses to lift up his hand and divide the waters. In between the death of the first born and the parting of the Red Sea, Moses had died to himself and began to so trust in God that when the people complained he didn't start making excuses or telling the people what he was going to do. Moses, for the first time, died to the point at which he didn't even consider what he was going to do to solve the problem. His only resource was God. His only power was in God. His only deliverance was in God. This change was so extreme and so complete that God was able to give authority to Moses. We often say that God split the Red Sea so Israel could cross upon dry ground. But if we read the text, we find God told Moses to part the sea. But this authority and power was not given until after Moses had a spiritual death experience.

Samson

Samson is one of the best-known characters in the Bible. He killed thousands. He married Delilah. He tormented the Philistines until his pride got the best of him and he told Delilah how to remove his strength. He is captured, tortured blinded and made to grind grain in a mill. Until one day when the Philistines were praising their god and mocking Samson and the God of Israel. At that moment, Samson can take no more mocking and cries out to God in Judges 16:28-30:

28 Then Samson called out to Adonai and said, "My Lord Adonai, please remember me and please strengthen me only this once, O God, so that I may this once take revenge on the Philistines for my two eyes."

29 Then Samson grasped the two middle pillars on which the temple rested and leaned on them, one with his right hand and the other with his left. 30 Then Samson said, "Let me die with the Philistines!" He bent with all his might so that the temple fell on the lords and on all the people who were in it. So the dead whom he killed at his death were more than those whom he killed during his life.

Samson's death was both spiritual and physical.

Peter

Peter is a favorite Biblical character as his humanity is always visible. From the first time we meet him as a fisherman to that moment when Yeshua asks, "Who do you say that I am?" followed by Peters response, "You are the Messiah, the Son of the Living God." Peter chopped the ear off of the arresting soldier of Yeshua. The Bible is very transparent about the mind and heart of Peter. Full of zeal, there is never any doubt of his assurance in his faith all the way until the crucifixion. At that moment, Peter's faith begins to wane and he is tested. Asked about his relationship with Yeshua, he denies the Lord three times. Then suddenly as we read in Luke 22:61- 62:

61 And the Lord turned and looked straight at Peter. Then Peter remembered the word of the Lord, how He had told him, 'Before the rooster crows today, you will deny Me three times.' 62 And Peter went out and wept bitterly.

Instantly, Peter is reminded of his proclamation found in Matthew 26:35:

35 "Even if I must die with You," Peter says to Him, "I'll never deny You!" And so said all the disciples.

Just hours before the execution of Yeshua, Peter with complete conviction and boldness proclaims he would never deny Yeshua. Yet when the time came, when the question of his commitment to being a disciple was asked, he not only denies Yeshua, but he denies him three times in the strongest possible way by swearing. Then suddenly the rooster crowed.

I can imagine Peter hearing both conversations running on continuous repeat in his mind. The guilt had to be overwhelming. But this pain led to the submission and spiritual death required to bring Peter to the place where he could be used by God.

Eric

From the moment I realized my attempts at ministry toward my mother were much more focused upon my desires, my will and my feelings than they were on Yeshua and God's, I understood I had forgotten God loved my mother and wanted my mother to love Him and accept Yeshua as her Messiah even more than I did. He had a plan for reaching her that included me but was not about me. It was even possible He did not require my involvement at all.

The understanding that I had focused on myself, my ideas, my intellect as if God was incapable of drawing my mother to faith in the same way he had drawn me, was shocking to my spirit. I had become so self-important I believed that my

171

mother's eternity was dependent on my figuring out the best way to reach her heart with the message of Yeshua.

You would think that after being hit by such a nuclear-powered revelation about myself, I would have responded by falling on my face and repenting of my self-idolatry. The truth is I did repent and spent quite a bit of time in tears, broken and repentant. I received the clear message that God didn't need my direct involvement to reach my mother. As a matter of fact, He had brought millions of people to relationship with Himself without my saying a single word to them.

I understood this truth and repented (turned directions). However, although I knew he didn't need my personal involvement to impact my mother with the Good News, I still felt that somehow I was responsible for her salvation. After all, God had given me a promise and I was going to make sure it came to pass.

As a result, my efforts changed from personal witnessing and sharing to attempting to reach her through other believers. I set up "chance meetings." I Introduced her to "friends who wanted to meet her," sent her books "she might enjoy reading" and many other devices contrived to help out God.

My faith for my promise was strong. I understood God didn't require my personal involvement to speak and share with my mother. But my faith in God's ability to fulfill His promise without any help at all from me was not yet achieved. Then one day, in a moment, everything changed. I was humbled completely. In front of my mother, my brothers and my sisters, God chose to bring me to my knees in pure humility. I died to myself, my will, my plans, and my ideas.

I was so dramatically changed in that twinkling of an eye, from that moment on when challenged by overwhelming situations and circumstances, those around me heared me say a simple phrase. "I would not worry about it." This phrase has become my battle cry against myself rising from the dead to try to do those things that we should always depend on God to do.

That phrase doesn't mean that whatever is happening isn't important. Those moments can be the most important.

But those words remind me I am responsible for turning to God and allow Him to rule and reign. To remember I am merely a private in His army, following his direction. These words keep me from trying to put His crown on my head again. Something I hope and pray I never do anymore.

The Death Questions

1) What does death to one's self look like?

2) Can you think of a "death" experience in your life?

3) Is death to self a one-time thing?

4) Is there anything you know today you need to die to self about?

5) What helps you keep the dead buried in your life?

The Promise Fulfilled

The final stage of the Pattern is the promise fulfilled. In the case of the criminal on the cross, his promise was "Amen, I tell you, today you shall be with Me in Paradise." In reading the narrative, we find that promise was fulfilled as that day this man passed from this world to the world to come. In this section we will review the same eight biblical figures and see if the pattern is consistent in this stage also.

Adam

As we review Adam's promises fulfilled, let's remember we pointed out two different promises given to Adam. The first promise was: Genesis 2:17:

17 But of the Tree of the Knowledge of Good and Evil you must not eat. For when you eat from it, you most assuredly will die!

This promise is fulfilled in **Genesis 5:5 So all Adam's**

days that he lived were 930 years, and then he died.

God kept his promise to Adam and Adam died. Some might say he didn't immediately die because he lived a long life. While that is true, we must remember without eating from the tree, Adam would never have died, so it wasn't an immediate death, but it was an immediate fulfillment. However, it is the second promise Adam received I want to focus upon because this promise shows us much more about God's love for his creation: Genesis 3:15:

15 I will put animosity between you and the woman— between your seed and her seed. He will crush your head, and you will crush his heel.

This promise of victory is the reason we have hope for redemption as it was based upon this promise that ultimately Yeshua was born, lived, died and rose again, crushing the head of the enemy. Galatians 4:4:

But when the fullness of time came, God sent out His Son, born of a woman and born under law—

Thousands of years transpired between Adam's day and Yeshua's, so how was Adam's promise fulfilled for Adam during his life? Genesis 4:25:

25 Adam was intimate with his wife again, and she gave birth to a son and she named him Seth, "For God has appointed me another seed in place of Abel—since Cain killed him." 26 To Seth, also was born a son. He named him Enosh. Then people began to call on Adonai's Name.

After they are cast out of the Garden of Eden, Adam and Eve have three sons Cain, Able and Seth. These three sons are the fulfillment of this second promise during Adam's life, as each of them is part of the continuing promise, which is ultimately brought to complete fulfillment in Yeshua. The fact that Adam and Eve had relations, bringing forth more children after being cast out of the garden, shows us that Adam had died to self, allowing the opening of the door to promise fulfillment brought forth through Eve's seed.

The fulfillment of God's promise to Abraham is found in Genesis 21:1-5:

1 Then Adonai visited Sarah just as He had said, and Adonai did for Sarah just as He had spoken. 2 So Sarah became pregnant and gave birth to a son for Abraham in his old age, at the appointed time that God had told him. 3 Abraham named his son who was born to him—whom Sarah bore for him—Isaac. 4 Then Abraham circumcised Isaac, his eight-day-old son, just as God had commanded him. 5 Abraham was 100 years old when Isaac his son was born to him.

Abraham is one of the clearest examples of the Pattern of blessing we can find. Once Abraham submitted himself to God's promises and quit trying to help God out with his ideas and got out of the way, he was able to receive his promised son, and 41 generations later, Yeshua was born.

Jacob

Jacob's promise is fulfilled in a unique way by God as we read in Genesis 33:4:

4 But Esau ran to meet him, hugged him, fell on his neck and kissed him—and they wept.

This greeting from his brother, which demonstrates God's promise to bring him home safely, shows Jacob the faithfulness of God.

But the fulfillment of promise doesn't just end with Esau's hug and kiss of welcome. As we continue to read, we find Esau upon Jacob's presentation of his "peace offering," says the following to his brother:

Genesis 33:8-9:

8 "What do you mean by this whole caravan that I've met?" So he said, "To find favor in your eyes, my lord." 9 But Esau said, "I have plenty! O my brother, do keep all that belongs to you."

180

Of course if we read through verse 11 we find that after Jacob pressures Esau, he does take the gift offered. But, what Esau says to his brother in verse 9 is significant. Jacob has just arrived home after 20 years away. He ran from his brother because he had deceived his father Isaac into giving him Esau's blessing. Esau then greets his brother with a hug and a kiss, showing forgiveness. He tells Jacob he should, "Keep all that belongs to him." This simple phrase showed forgiveness and ultimately demonstrated the fulfillment of God's promise more than the hug and kiss.

It is after this meeting that Jacob receives the promises he received when he first left Canaan: the promise of the land, given first to his grandfather, Abraham; the continuing "seed promise" which was given to Adam; the promise of God's presence in his life wherever he travels; the promise God would watch over him protecting him; the promise God would bring him back to the covenant land; the promise God would never forsake him.

Joseph

The promise given to Joseph through dreams was in two parts. The first dream was Genesis 37:7:

7 There we were binding sheaves in the middle of the field. All of a sudden, my sheaf arose and stood upright. And behold, your sheaves gathered around and bowed down to my sheaf."

This described Joseph's brothers bowing down before him, which is fulfilled in Genesis 42:7-8:

7 Then Joseph's brothers came and bowed down to him with faces to the ground. When Joseph saw his brothers, he recognized them, but he made himself unrecognizable to them. Then he spoke harshly and said to them, "Where have you come from?" "From the land of Canaan," they said, "to buy grain as food."
8 Though Joseph recognized his brothers, they did not recognize him.

The second dream is in Genesis 37:9-10:

9 But then he dreamed another dream and told it to his brothers, saying, "I have just dreamed another dream. Suddenly, there was the sun and the moon and the eleven stars bowing down to me!" 10 He told it to his father as well as his brothers. Then his father rebuked him and said to him, "What's this dream you dreamed? Will we really come—your mother and I with your brothers—to bow down to the ground to you?"

Which is fulfilled in Genesis 46:31:

31 Then Joseph said to his brothers and to his father's household, "I'll go up and tell Pharaoh, and say to him, 'My brothers and my father's household who were in the land of Canaan have come to me.

Joseph speaks with authority to his brothers and to his father's household, although he submitted to his father. His father's household was under Joseph's authority as viceroy of Egypt.

The following verse bears this out as Joseph continues to instruct on what they must do when they meet Pharaoh.

Moses

The promise to Moses is in Exodus Chapter 14:21-22:

21 Then Moses stretched out his hand over the sea. Adonai drove the sea back with a strong east wind throughout the night and turned the sea into dry land. So the waters were divided. 22 Then Bnei-Yisrael went into the midst of the sea on the dry ground, while the waters were like walls to them on their right and on their left.

As the Children of Israel stepped onto the dry ground of the Red Sea, Moses' promise was fulfilled. God promised Moses he would bring His people out of Egypt and once they moved into the sea, they were out of Egypt. Of course they had a long trip ahead of them and many more promises to be fulfilled, but Moses's promise was complete.

Judges 13:5 lets us know of the promise placed upon Samson's life and, although he had more than his share of detours between the promise being made and it being fulfilled, his promise was fulfilled.

5 For behold, you will conceive and bear a son. Let no razor come upon his head, for the boy will be a Nazirite to God from the womb. He will begin to deliver Israel from the hand of the Philistines.

Samson's promise came to fullness just before his death in similar fashion to the criminal on the cross.

In Judges 16:30:

30 Then Samson said, "Let me die with the Philistines!" He bent with all his might so that the temple fell on the lords and on all the people who were in it. So the dead whom he killed at his death were more than those whom he killed during his life.

With one mighty push, Samson began the deliverance of Israel from the hands of the Philistines. In his death, Samson's prayers were answered and God's promise was brought forth. It didn't happen in a way we would consider joyful, but if we could have heard Samson's final thoughts as the pillars broke and the temple fell on his enemies, I would think for him it was filled with joy and peace.

Peter

Looking at Peter's promise or rather promises, we noted three of them in the promises section. The first was concerning Peter's receiving the "Keys to the Kingdom," the second and third were about Peter both falling away and then returning or repenting.

As we look at the fulfillment of Peter's promises, let's look first at the second promise.

The promise of Peter falling away was evident when Yeshua said that Peter would deny Him three times before the cock crowed. In Luke 22:60-62:

60 But Peter said, "Man, I don't know what you're talking about!" And immediately, while he was still speaking, a rooster crowed. 61 And the Lord turned and looked straight at Peter. Then Peter remembered the word of the Lord, how He had told him, 'Before the rooster crows today, you will deny Me three times.' 62 And Peter went out and wept bitterly.

We read of both Peter's falling away and third denial of Yeshua, and his repentance in verse 62, when he wept bitterly at the revelation that even though he had promised Yeshua he would never deny Him, he had fallen. He had to be remembering his earlier statement in Luke 22:33:

33 But Simon said to Him, "Master, I am ready to go with You even to prison and to death!"

This promise was made and brought about in Peter's life within hours in such a dramatic way. However, the first promise we discussed didn't come to pass for months from when Yeshua spoke it over Peter. Yeshua told Peter in Matthew 16:19:

19 I will give you the keys of the kingdom of heaven. Whatever you forbid on earth will have been forbidden in heaven and what you permit on earth will have been permitted in heaven."

This promise begins fulfillment in Acts Chapter 2 when Peter preaches the message of the Good News to the Jewish people gathered on Shavuot or Pentecost. It continues as Peter preaches to the Samaritans after he is called, sent by the emissaries as we read in Acts 8:14-17:

14 Now when the emissaries in Jerusalem heard that Samaria had accepted the message of God, they sent Peter and John to them. 15 They came down and prayed for them to receive the Ruach ha-Kodesh.
16 For He had not yet come upon them; they had only been immersed in the name of the Lord Yeshua.
17 Then they began laying their hands on them, and they were receiving the Ruach ha-Kodesh.

The promise is completed when Peter is called by Cornelius, a Gentile and Peter turns the Keys to the Kingdom again in Acts 10:44-47:

44 While Peter was still speaking these words, the Ruach ha-Kodesh fell on all those hearing the message. 45 All the circumcised believers who came with Peter were astonished, because the gift of the Ruach ha-Kodesh had been poured out even on the Gentiles. 46 For they were hearing them speaking in tongues and magnifying God. Then Peter answered, 47"Can anyone refuse water for these to be immersed, who have received the Ruach ha-Kodesh just as we did?"

The Keys given to Peter first unlocked the message of Yeshua as Messiah to the Jews, then the Samaritans and Gentiles. Fulfilling Adonai's promise, Peter went to each people group and used the Keys to the Kingdom to unlock the door to the message of redemption through Messiah Yeshua, and with the turning of the key there was a powerful move of the Ruach HaKodesh.

Eric

I know in the section about death, I abruptly stopped without clearly showing the moment or event that brought about my spiritual death to self in the story of my mother's death. I did this for a reason and that is because the death experience was so integrated with my promise fulfilled, that in order to explain, I had to first share the next stage of the Pattern and then look backward into the moment of "death."

As I began this book, I was sharing about the personal struggle I was having with my mother's sudden sickness and death. As with most people, death is difficult to experience, even if you are a person of faith. Loss of a loved one is traumatic, even with a long period of time to emotionally prepare. When someone suddenly passes the loss and pain seem to be multiplied to family and friends.

This loss can be even more dramatic for a person who believes that one must have a relationship with Yeshua as Messiah in order to live eternally with God. When this happens, the loss becomes more than just a death it can become an eternal loss.

My mother, the centerpiece of my family, was in a hospital bed suffering from the horrors of cancer, which seemed to have attacked her only weeks before. Her body was now weak but her mind was sharp as ever. We all knew she had only hours or at the most, days to live. I had to know where she was spiritually. It is hard to explain that although I had never heard my mother express her faith in Yeshua, I had no doubt that somehow, someway she was going to come to faith.

My wondering about her relationship with God was not because I was concerned she would not come to faith. It was only a matter of wondering how God was going to do what He had promised. Another way to say this is, I knew she was going to come to faith in Yeshua; I didn't know how she was going to come to faith. My curiosity was based in being interested in the how, not the if.

When the time was right, along with my two brothers and sister in the hospice room, I asked my mother this question. "Mom, you know time is short and I would like to know where you are spiritually."
She replied, "I want to have a Messianic Jewish Funeral."

I asked her, "What does that mean?"

Not wanting to put words into her mouth, I asked, "Does that just mean you want me to do the service?"

She replied, "No. It means I believe in Yeshua as my Messiah."

Trying to limit the outward expression of my excitement, while at the same time trying to find out what brought her to the conclusion that Yeshua was the Messiah, I asked, "Mom, what brought you to decide to believe?"

Her answer was so simple and so sincere. No theological statement that I could use in sharing with others in the future, no deeply spiritual vision or dream that would make a great sermon anecdote. She just said, "It was the only thing that made sense."

Here was a moment where I was surrounded by unanswered questions that swirled around my mind with almost nothing about the past two weeks making sense to me, and my mom's answer to the most important question in life, was that believing in Yeshua just made the most sense.

It was at that moment with those words that I received my promise from God. My mother had become a believer in Yeshua. When? I didn't know. How? I didn't know. What verse or verses helped her reach the conclusion? I didn't know. Was it a sermon or a book? I didn't know. At this same time, I also experienced my "death to self" experience. I died to myself.

What was most amazing, although I was the rabbi, it was my mother who preached a one sentence message that brought me to faith. Her short statement about making sense was the straw that broke the camel's back in my wrestling match with God.

Until that moment in time, while I completely believed God would keep every one of His promises, I still had not stopped believing that somehow, I was important to the process. The truth is, God makes sense. He always makes sense and if it doesn't appear He is making sense, it is not Him, it is us. I didn't need a plan, I didn't need a script. I didn't need to do anything other than believe the perfect God would make perfect sense.

Now I know that this may seem simple and elementary but many times we are straining to see the complex, when the simple holds the key to our problems. For you, the last gasp of breath as you submit to the total will and direction of God will be unique. It may be simple. I can assure you it will be a powerful moment or reality that will change your world view. I cannot tell you what it will be or how it will come about. For me, it was a few words spoken by my mother. If you want to walk in the fullness of God's promises, the pattern shared in this book is the way that it will come about.

I began this book saying that I left my mom's room with many "whys." Every one of those questions were answered when I learned this pattern.

On our last morning together, I entered my mother's room and asked, "How are you feeling?"
"I am wonderful!" she replied. "I spent all last night talking with my Messiah."

Those words rang joyfully in my ears, as I searched for all of the "whys" I asked myself after her death. Her answer to my question about Yeshua was the answer I ultimately came to for my questions. It is the only thing that makes sense. God's word is not arbitrary. It holds the answers to life and blessings. We just need to follow the Pattern, and when we do, suddenly everything will make sense.

Promised Fulfilled Questions

1) Make a list of the promises God fulfilled in your life.

2) Looking back at those promises, can you identify the stages of this pattern in each one?

3) Now that you see the pattern, do you think it will help you identify where you are to better help you walk in blessings?

4) Since beginning this study, have you received a promise fulfilled?

5) Try to identify where in the pattern you are in relationship to the promises you have yet to receive?

Made in the USA
Middletown, DE
09 April 2022